Shaman, M.D.

To my Mother Fay and Father Marvin through whose union I was born.
To Mother Earth and Father Sky through whose union I live.

Shaman, M.D.

A Plastic Surgeon's Remarkable Journey
into the World of Shapeshifting

Eve Bruce, M.D.

Destiny Books
Rochester, Vermont

Destiny Books
One Park Street
Rochester, Vermont 05767
www.InnerTraditions.com

Destiny Books is a division of Inner Traditions International

The story in this book reflects my life as I recall it. To enhance the flow of the narrative or to emphasize certain concepts, some of the details of this story have been changed, and actual events may have occurred in a different chronological order. Some names have been changed and some characters and conversations are composites of real people and events.

The section of chapter 5 entitled "Entering the Circle of Yachaks" appeared first in *Magical Blend* magazine.

Library of Congress Cataloging-in-Publication Data

Bruce, Eve, 1954-
    Shaman, M.D. : a plastic surgeon's remarkable journey into the world
of shapeshifting / Eve Bruce.
    p. ; cm.
    ISBN 0-89281-976-6
    1. Bruce, Eve, 1954- . 2. Plastic surgeons—United States—Biography.
3. Shamanism—Ecuador.
    [DNLM: 1. Alternative Medicine—Personal Narratives. 2.
Shamanism—Personal Narratives. 3. Surgery, Plastic—Personal Narratives.
WB 890 B886s 2002] I. Title.
    RD27.35.B78 A3 2002
    617.9'5'092—dc21
                                        2001006311

Printed and bound in Canada

10 9 8 7 6 5 4 3 2 1

Text design and layout by Crystal Roberts and Priscilla Baker
This book was typeset in Caslon, with Reiner Script and Gill Sans as display typefaces

Contents

Acknowledgments   vi

Introduction   I

One: Looking Outside the Box   17

Two: The Dream Called Doctor   27

Three: Choose Your Dream—Create Your World   40

Four: Trees across the River of Life   52

Five: The Path of the Shaman   74

Six: Cultural Collisions   97

Seven: Remembered Wellness—   118
          Dreaming a New Vision of Health

Eight: Shapeshifting Our Lives   139

Epilogue: Coming Home to the Great Mother   167

Acknowledgments

As you read this book and swim through the river of folly that is my life, you will understand that many are my teachers and that it is way beyond the scope of this page to even begin to acknowledge everyone. Yet I shall begin, and I apologize in advance for my omissions.

First and foremost I want to acknowledge John Perkins, a teacher and friend, whose unflagging energy and dedication to his vision of a world where we take action to honor all sentient beings, inspired me in the first place to look outside the box, and continues to inspire me to stretch further and further. To give thanks to my mother and father who gave me the gift of life. To my children Alice, Michael, Coale, and Jock and my granddaughters Blake, Morgan, and Olivia, who teach me in so many ways. To Ipupiara and Cleicha. To don Esteban, Jorge, and Jose Tamayo. To Maria Juana Yamberla. To Daniel Wachapa. To the Arcos family. To Jose Joaquin and Soraya Pineda. To Mercedes Barrios Longfellow and Gerrardo Barrios. To Vusamazulu Credo Mutwa. To Alberto and Elva Tatzo. To Running Water. To Wolf. To Ann Bell. To Thuptan Lamaji. To Elizabeth Kramer. To Juan Gabriel Carrasco. To Shruthi Mahalingaiah. To Paula and Mitch Liester. To Sheena Singh. To Mary Tendall and Lyn Roberts-Herrick. To Robert Levy, Vickie Novak, Bob Southard, Wendi Whitsett, Angela Vaughan Clark, and so many other DCC members.

To all of my workshop and trip participants, patients, and coworkers.

To life, to every breath, every situation, every friend and foe, to the rain, the ocean, the sun, the moon, the earth, the mountains, the wind, the fire, the plants, the trees, the birds, the animals, the bacteria and viruses, the colors, the scents, the tastes, the textures. To the music of each moment of my life. To all these teachers.

I want to give a special thanks to Laura Schlivek and Nancy Yeilding, who patiently and lovingly molded and worked the material, creating from it a real book.

Introduction

June 2000—Deep in the Amazon Jungle

JOURNEYING IN DREAMTIME, I sat in a trance opposite the Shuar shaman Wachapa while he chanted prayers of healing and connection. When he stopped chanting I shivered, returning to the physical world. The oppressive heat of the day had turned to a cold, dark night—thick, black, impenetrable darkness, the glowing embers of the perpetual Shuar fire providing the only discernible visual sensation. Without the distraction of eyesight, my other senses jumped to active attention. Thunderous rain beat incessantly on the rooftop, on the canopy of trees, and on the earth of the clearing. We were in the "round room," the area reserved for visitors from Dream Change Coalition—an association of Westerners and indigenous people that promotes reconnecting with indigenous wisdom as a way to rebalance Mother Earth.

A traditional Shuar lodge is made of vertical bamboo slats arranged so that no one can see in, but it is easy to look out and observe possible intruders. The lodges are thatched, with a carefully prepared hard-packed dirt floor divided into a "male" area where guests are received and a "female" area where no one other than family may enter. A fire is kept burning at all times; it is used for cooking and for warmth, to cure the roof and keep it free from insects and rodents, and especially to provide a pathway for spirits near the central pole.

The round room where we were sitting is also a lodge, modified for Westerners and designed for easy upkeep as it is not always inhabited. The construction is very similar to that of a traditional lodge, but it is almost completely open—a dirt floor covered by a thatched roof, with more than one pole to accommodate a group of hammocks, benches formed from old dugout canoes around the edges, and no male/female separation for our transient visiting family. The round room provided us a place to lie in a hammock and bask in the air of the jungle during the daytime and a place to hold healing ceremonies at night.

I took a deep breath, inhaling the ripe, wet scent of the jungle, mingled with the wood smoke in the lodge, the acrid smell of tobacco soaking in a cup nearby, and the heady vapors rising from an open bottle of *trago*, a sugarcane alcohol. I tuned in to the energy of the man across from me, the shaman Daniel Wachapa, in deep trance under the influence of *ayahuasca*, the sacred teacher plant. As he resumed chanting, I sank back on the bench and found myself dreaming again. Awakening with a start, I pulled my shirt tighter against the cold. The rain had stopped and the full moon slipped out from under a cover of clouds in the clearing. Now the jungle was singing with the familiar cacophony of animal music. Life pulsed, and in the distance a jaguar roared. It was time. I sensed this from the shaman just before he called to me to ask if anyone would like to come forward for a healing. I translated his invitation to the group seated in anticipation around the lodge, some drifting in and out of ayahuasca-induced visions, their assigned buddies ready to assist as conscious guides at any moment.

Someone called my name from the clearing. Wading through puddles to answer the call, I found Beth, an internist from New England, standing in the shimmering moonlight with her buddy Dave, who had summoned me. Beth had all the trappings of success in the United States: a busy medical practice, three children in private schools, a sprawling home in the suburbs, and a vacation home at the beach. Successful, wealthy, attractive, intelligent, admired by all who came in contact with her—why was she out here in the jungle staring fixedly at the sky? She had been vomiting profusely and appeared to have purged completely. *

---

*Sacred to the Shuar for its ability to provide contact with the spirit world, ayahuasca will never be a recreational drug—before reaping its benefits, those who take it must endure severe nausea, vomiting, and diarrhea.

Dave spoke to me in whispers to avoid startling Beth or disturbing her visions. He said she was ready to go before the shaman for a healing. I touched her shoulder gently and held her softly. "What do you see?" I whispered into her ear.

"A giant anaconda," Beth answered. "It's coiled up over there." She pointed to a space in the distance. "Now it's coming after me. I'm scared!" she exclaimed, grabbing my hand. "It's up there now," she said, pointing to the air in front of her, "and it's opening its mouth. It's huge!"

"I'm here," I reminded her. "Go to it. Move into your fear. Reach out and touch it. Ask it why it has come to you. Ask what it brings." As she moved hesitantly forward, I saw her reach her arm outward and upward. The fear clearly present in her face, she turned to me, determined and strong, and then turned back and reached further to touch the vision of the snake. She asked the questions firmly with courage. Her face softened instantly, a smile grew on her lips, and her eyes lit up in a way I hadn't seen before in her.

"What did he tell you?" I asked. "What did he bring?"

"He came to bring my soul back," Beth stated with conviction. "He came to bring me back my feet so that I may walk again." Smiling broadly, she turned toward the lodge, and Dave and I led her to the bench where the shaman waited, chanting in ecstatic trance.

I helped Beth lie down in front of Wachapa, who had moved to the turtle stool, a symbol of Tsunqui, the goddess of the river, known as the first shaman in Shuar lore. I removed Beth's shirt, and she lay down in the dark, lost again in her visions. The shaman began. Praying and chanting for assistance, he entered the spirit world in order to see Beth in a different way, sending in invisible darts, *tsentsak,* to find problems and act as tools for extraction. Sitting next to him, I watched as he leaned forward toward her heart and began the extraction, sucking on the skin over the area where he had seen a problem. Time melted as the work continued. Wachapa continued to suck, extracting more and more. From time to time he would stop and retch violently, vomiting out the concretized energy and sending it into the earth to flow into a new form. He pointed to the ground in front of him to show me something. This time the extracted energy had solidified into a bone. He leaned forward with renewed determination and concluded the extraction. Wachapa's wife, who sat at his side, announced the arrival of the spirits Tsunqui and Amaruu. Like Tsunqui, Amaruu is very important to Shuar shamans and is the name used for the spirit of the anaconda, the anaconda itself being known as Pangi. Amaruu is a particularly strong spirit guide for Wachapa, an ally I have seen him use on many occasions.

Turning to his tools, Wachapa grasped the bundle of leaves that he had gathered earlier in the forest and began to shake them all over Beth's body, producing a "tsing-tsing" sound as he shook. *Tsing-tsing* is the onomatopoeic name of the plant that he was using in healing; the shaking leaves made a music that connected all who could hear it to the spirit of the plant world. Through Wachapa's deep connection with spirit and the world around him, his journeying in trance, his prayer through chanting, and his cleansing with the tsing-tsing leaves, he completed Beth's healing and restored the integrity of her soul, returning her to flow and balance.

Dave helped Beth back to her room and stayed with her through the night while she continued her dreams and visions. I called to Juan Gabriel Carrasco, my spiritual brother and partner, and we looked around for the next person ready for healing.

Juan Gabriel and I lead groups of people to visit indigenous shamans in the Andes and the Amazon River basin of Ecuador for Dream Change Coalition. Dream Change was the brainchild of John Perkins, a successful businessman and a consultant to Fortune 500 companies and the World Bank. John had apprenticed with the Shuar in the late 1960s when he was stationed in the Ecuadorian Amazon as a Peace Corps volunteer. His ostensible purpose was to instruct the impoverished Shuar in the development of savings and loan cooperatives, but he soon discovered that they had nothing to save, nothing to loan, and no desire to take more from Mother Earth than they needed to survive.

Though the Shuar communities were impoverished by Western standards of material wealth, they were incomparably rich in their ecstatic knowing of the oneness of all life. They lived each moment fully in spirit, connected to the earth and to each other and aware of the power of their dreams. It was the Shuar shaman Numi who taught John that "the world is as you dream it," which became the title of one of John's many acclaimed books. John also discovered the richness of the Shuar's healing abilities when he became so sick that he was near death, too weak to walk for days to the nearest "civilized" area to get medical care. Shaman Numi came forward to save his life, and it was then that John understood that he had come not to teach, but to learn. He apprenticed with Numi and became a shaman himself.

Returning to the community twenty years later, John found an area stripped of trees and of spirit. Going deeper into the jungle, he found many of his Shuar friends, and he asked the shamans what he could do to give something back. As a result of his meetings with the shamans, John started Dream Change Coalition in the early 1990s. Building from the Shuar understanding that the world is as we dream it, Dream Change Coalition helps us look at our dreams and at the world that has come out of them. Dream Change asks us to reassess and to collectively dream our future according to its three basic tenets: taking steps to change the dream of industrialized societies to a sustainable, earth-honoring one; making efforts to preserve forests and other natural areas; and making use of indigenous wisdom to foster social and environmental balance.*

Like John Perkins, when I first came to the Shuar, I found a community rich in passion, in knowledge, in connection, and in shamanic healing abilities. I also came to realize that I wanted to study the ways of these master healers and to bring others who were interested in learning what indigenous viewpoints have to teach us. Four years before, I had been a physician very similar to Beth on a Dream Change trip with John Perkins, Joyce Ferranti, and Juan Gabriel. Like Beth, the outer trappings of my life were impressive, desirable, and even seductive. Yet there was something very wrong, something missing from my life, which seemed to have taken a path that left my soul far behind in the dust.

---

*For more about the Shuar, John Perkins, and Dream Change Coalition, see *The World Is As You Dream It* by John Perkins (Destiny Books, 1994) and *Spirit of the Shuar* by John Perkins and Shakaim Mariano Chumpi (Destiny Books, 2001).

After four years of participation in Dream Change Coalition, my soul soared. I felt more complete and in possession of greater riches than the "great American dream" could ever have given me because following that dream meant that my soul could not be aligned with my path. I had found a passion in life and a community within Dream Change Coalition that functioned like a tribe, with all the joy and support that community brings. Helping Beth to reconnect with her soul and its purpose was a way to give back some of what Dream Change and the shamans had given me.

The next morning the shaman spoke with Beth and Dave as I translated. "How do you feel?" he asked them both. Dave answered first. "Terrific! I never understood before that helping someone else through such a deeply transformative experience could actually be of benefit to me. I feel like I was the one getting the healing."

"Yes," replied Wachapa, "the ecstatic experience is for everyone. We are all one, and when one is healed, we are all healed." He went on to explain that when we move into the spiritual experience of our lives and bodies, we find a deep connection—with the forest, with the animals, with the earth, with spirit, and with each other.

"I want to keep this feeling forever!" said Dave.

"Why not?" I answered. "Choose that as your dream and make it so."

Beth turned to Wachapa, smiling. "Thank you," she said, as I continued translating. "I can't describe what happened, but I feel like a new person. I'm actually excited about the day ahead, about tomorrow, about getting back to my children, about living. I haven't felt like this for so long that I can't even remember the last time I did."

Beth went on to say that she felt she had been blindsided, so consumed by her dream of success that it had taken control of her and begun to take on a life of its own. She remembered the anaconda telling her that she had her feet back. To Beth that meant that she could choose her own path and walk consciously. "I suddenly feel that I can see much further," she said. "I see my life ahead of me and behind me and my connection to all of earth and the cosmos. I got my soul back!"

Months later she called to tell me how things had gone since our night together in the jungle. Before the trip she had been diagnosed with breast cancer and had undergone a mastectomy. The diagnosis and surgery had shaken her deeply. Suddenly she'd felt lost in her own world. Everything she thought she knew was called into question. But she said that since her healing in the jungle she had continued to feel a renewed excitement and passion for life and a deep sense of her eternal spirit and oneness with the rest of creation.

"Nothing has changed about my life if you look from the outside," she said. "I still have the same problems, the same home and work. Yet everything has changed. I feel well in every way. I even feel pretty, something I haven't experienced for many years, since long before the surgery. My children feel it; we've had incredible conversations. I always thought that heaven would be a place without challenge; lots of sunshine, a beach with warm water, and plenty of delicacies to eat that would never make you gain a pound! Don't laugh," she said, as I began to giggle.

"I'm not laughing at you, I am laughing at me," I said. "I used to think the same thing—that life now was difficult, but that if you were as good as you could be, later you would find a heaven, after death, and in heaven there would be no challenges. The Shuar see life completely differently. They live connected to spirit every moment of their physical lives and listen to the messages of their dreams, their environment, their bodies, and their situations very carefully."

I reminded Beth that the Shuar not only know that they have the power to dream their own realities; they also know that heaven is a choice. To the Shuar, imagining a life without ecstasy, passion, and challenge—without deep connection to the earth, the spirits, the elements, their dreams, and one another—would be to imagine a fate far worse than death. To them, death is just another shapeshift, one in which they will nourish others as others have nourished them, freeing them to go on to another life—as a human, an animal, or the rain. "To live in ecstasy, as they do," I said, "is to live fully and passionately in this physical life every moment, embodying your spirit fully and feeling deeply the interconnectedness of your dreams with the dreams of everyone else."

"I knew all that intellectually," answered Beth, laughing along with me, "but now I feel it in my heart. After experiencing ecstasy, the knowing that we are all one, I consciously choose to live in ecstasy forever, understanding that heaven is a choice, here and now."

July 2000—Operating Room, Aesthetic Institute of Maryland, Timonium, Maryland

She looked so beautiful as she lay there without worries, no tension in her anesthetically paralyzed muscles, a deep sleeping tranquility on her face. She looked both beautiful and young, and I loved putting in those last few sutures, knowing the long day of work was almost over, enjoying the feeling of a job well done.

I had been in the operating room for eight hours. Hungry, my feet tired, I looked forward to sitting down to eat and dictating the day's procedures. First I needed to finish stitching the skin of the facelift and put on the dressing. The light bright from overhead, my headlamp adding an additional spot beam, the magnifying loupes narrowing my field of vision and magnifying the tiny sutures to four times their size, I concentrated on rearranging the skin, trimming around the ear, and closing the wound. As we wrapped up the procedure, our team of four found ourselves relaxing and telling jokes. The Dixie Chicks sang loud in the background, and we joined in with the refrain "Hello Mr. Heartache . . ."

Mary had come into my office six months earlier for a consultation. Recently divorced, she wanted to have facial rejuvenation surgery before she celebrated her fiftieth birthday. Her request was not unusual in the realm of plastic surgery. I had treated hundreds of similar cases.

We went through her medical history and I examined her clinically. I asked her why she wanted the surgery, what she hoped to accomplish by it. We discussed the many surgical options available, the procedures, the alternatives, the expected recovery, the risks, and possible complications. Then I returned to my first question, explaining that it was the most important question I had asked. "Why? Why are you contemplating this surgery, this change in your body?" I told Mary that I could not answer this question for her, but that I ask all my patients to spend time exploring their motivations in any way in which they feel comfortable.

We talked about the body and the spirit, about our lives and passions, about our dreams. I explained to her that since she had come to me asking for change, it followed that this was the perfect time to clarify what change meant to her. Whether she decided to go ahead with the surgery or not, the more clarity she could gain about her hopes, her definition of change, and what she was searching for—whether she hoped to regain something lost or find something she had always aspired to—the better the results would be.

I told her that I had watched many patients undergo plastic surgery and afterward shapeshift in every way: their bodies, their attitudes, their jobs, their relationships. Other patients had beautiful photographic results but became unhappy people with tighter skin, as if the surgery had been a misdirected dream. My experience has been that this disappointment with the results of surgery seems to happen more for people who say they don't want to be "vain," in other words, for people who devalue their physical bodies and physical dreams. I let Mary know that the more attuned she could become to her physical body and to her environment, the more connected she would be to all her hopes and dreams, physical and otherwise.

As I spoke to Mary, my assistant Pamela entered the room and remarked in her usual gentle manner, "My, you are so beautiful."

Mary burst into tears. "Oh no, I'm not. I was just sitting here wondering if I should give up. I'll never be pretty."

Pretty? Try drop-dead gorgeous! This woman could easily have doubled for Michelle Pfeiffer, but she was so disconnected from her body that she didn't think she was, or ever would be, pretty.

"You are absolutely correct," I said, astonishing her. I had gotten her attention, and she stopped crying to see what I meant.

"With that outlook, even if we operated every year you would never be pretty in your own eyes. Let's take a reality check. If I pulled one hundred people off the street and filed them through this room, asking each of them to describe you, they would all say that you are beautiful. If you are that disconnected from the reality of your physical body, you will never feel pretty."

I handed her a mirror, and she examined her image as if for the first time.

"You're right," she said. "I have never felt pretty, and when anyone tries to give me a compliment, I feel even worse. I do want change. I want to be pretty and to feel pretty, too."

Mary went through a great deal of soul-searching after that session and learned much about herself, her patterns, her disconnection, her dreams. She chose to have the facelift operation, and to follow her heart in changing her life in many other ways. She made a firm commitment to connect to her physical body, to her life, to her community—she would embody her spirit from then on. She realized that I could rearrange her skin, but it was up to her to take responsibility for rearranging her life and finding her mission. She shapeshifted her life, even before the surgery.

Upon hearing that I am both a shaman and a plastic surgeon, many people have a hard time understanding how I could work in both worlds while remaining true to myself, that is, while maintaining my integrity. My two roles sound to them like a contradiction in terms. Every day I hear people voice disdain for any physical dreams and aspirations. Patients apologize for being "vain" and "indulging" this vanity by coming to me to manifest their dreams. Even the words they use point to our culture's unspoken conviction that the physical is trivial and has nothing to do with the spiritual.

Through the years I have seen shamans shapeshift before my eyes into jaguars, anacondas, and volcanoes. I have also seen people of my own culture shapeshift their bodies by losing weight rapidly without effort, looking and feeling younger and more vital, changing their eye color, growing inches taller long after puberty, or recovering from mangling injuries after being told there is no hope of full surgical repair, among many other examples. Physical shapeshifts can be and are done all the time, although in our culture it often takes quite some time and effort to break down barriers. Too often, I have seen people complete a physical shapeshift and then continue to struggle emotionally, mentally, and spiritually.

Shamanic communities do not separate the physical from the spiritual in the way that we in Western cultures have since the days of Descartes. Through a very deep connection with their physical bodies and the physical environment, they truly embody their spirits. It is a great paradox of our time and culture that in order to effectively transcend our obsession with the materialistic aspects of life we need to fully embrace the physical. Instead of further disconnecting the physical from the spiritual by focusing solely on spirit (while devaluing everything that is physical), we need to connect to the physical in a much more profound way. We need to learn how to embody our spirits in this physical experience called life. It is in facilitating this connection that I am able to combine my seemingly opposing roles as plastic surgeon and shaman.

August 2000—Baltimore, Maryland

Grace was a middle-aged housewife who had chosen to have rhinoplasty (more commonly known as a "nose job") some years before with a plastic surgeon I had never met. She had been very unhappy with the results. In fact, the outcome of the surgery had been so far removed from her expectations that she had remained housebound for two years afterward, not wanting to go out in public where anyone could see her. She had slowly started coming out of her house again, but only to visit her family and select close friends. She had called me because she had heard about my shamanic workshops and wanted to explore her body image, her goals, her expectations, and her dreams before considering revisionary surgery.

From our initial conversation on the telephone, I expected to see someone who had been monstrously disfigured. When she arrived at my office, I saw a bitter, angry woman with a severe, determined—but handsome—face. No monster at all. But she had been crippled by the gap between her expectations and her perception of her surgical outcome. We did talk about the possibility of revisionary surgery, but we spent more time exploring Grace's extreme reaction to her first operation. From the moment that she asked for change by contemplating that first rhinoplasty, Grace had been at a gateway. Why had she experienced such difficulty with stepping through that gateway and manifesting both internal and external change?

I met with Grace several times and came to know her well. She was not crazy, but she was living a life vastly different from that of her childhood dreams. In fact, she had stopped dreaming for herself altogether. The nasal surgery had been a grasp at reclaiming her life and her passion. When she found that surgery alone could not offer deliverance, she had given up in despair.

As I continued to talk with Grace, she emerged as an extremely intelligent and receptive woman of great intuitive ability. But her intelligence and intuition were strengths that she had never valued. They had not been nurtured or allowed to develop fully within the confines of her current life in the suburbs. She was certainly frustrated, as well as bitter and withdrawn. Yet she had come. I knew that she had made a choice to change—her life, her looks, her relationship with the world, her reality. She was ready.

She came to be healed by me. Could I help her?

I was not sure. I had been witness to hundreds of shamanic healings and had taught many nonindigenous people to shapeshift their lives and bodies, to reassess and clarify their dreams. I had witnessed complete healing of many diseases through shamanic techniques: chronic back pain, migraine headaches, allergies, alcoholism, infertility, gender difficulties, cysts, tumors, and cancers, to name a few. But Grace was in denial—afraid, angry, and bitter. What is more, she felt these strong feelings in reaction to an operation that I perform frequently. Perhaps I was not the one to help her. Yet she had come to me. There are no coincidences. And I remembered the words of my friend and teacher Manolo, a great Andean shaman. "It is not us doing the healing," he said. "It is Pachamama."*

He continued, "When I was young my father taught me the ways of the Yachaks, healing in the shamanic ways. For many years I tried so hard to make all the symptoms go away. That was my primary focus and where I put my energy. One day my father came to me and asked me what would happen if I rid a person of his symptoms only to see him come down with

---

*Pachamama is the Quechua name for Mother Earth/universe/time—what my own father and other physicists know as the space-time continuum.

yet another, perhaps even worse, disease. What then? Slowly my focus became one of helping people reconnect with their spirits. I taught them to listen to the messages coming through their bodies, lives, and environments, and to flow in alignment with their soul's directions. I learned that sometimes disease is a necessary part of the overall healing. Ridding a person of symptoms is a nice benefit, but it is not the primary focus."

"I will help you," I told Grace.

Grace stood awkwardly before me in the in the middle of the healing room as I prepared the space, eyes closed and naked but for her swimsuit, which she had insisted upon wearing. Calling on my guides, I connected with the elemental healing forces—with Pachamama—to help her with her dream change. Burning the smoke of aromatic herbs and resins, I prepared the sacred objects *(huacas)* and flowers in the way of the ancient Incan Yachaks, the birdpeople shamans of the Andes. I called to spirit in her name to ask for assistance so that she could break down her barriers and align with her soul's mission. After rubbing a candle over her body to gather her energy, I lit the flame. The candle spoke of her problems, of her spirit, of her mind, of her heart, of her body. The "diagnostic" phase done, we moved on to the cleansing with eggs, flowers, tobacco, and huacas—stones from the sacred volcanoes, the Amazon, and the Indus that have stayed with me as guides, helpers, and friends for many years.

I asked Grace to connect deeply with her spirit, her body, and her dreams. I asked her to journey—to psychonavigate—and to feel her desired face, her desired life, her desired dream as a fait accompli, to bring the dream here and now—to shapeshift. Throughout the healing, my cleansing efforts were directed by my spirit guides to where energy was blocked, sluggish, or nonproductive for her. Using my tools to focus and assist, I extracted, brushed away, and infused. I encouraged Grace to feel the full energy of the change in her physical body and in her heart, mind, and spirit.

Although Grace had no previous shamanic experiences and no knowledge of psychonavigation, she found herself letting go and easily accessing her spiritual plane, connecting it to her physical. She spoke of how she felt immersed in the light and radiance of her own beauty, at one with her body and sensuality, connected to her religious background and to her divine creator.

As Grace dressed after the healing session, she smiled warmly, glowing, and we connected as one. She came for two more healings before she was willing to consider appearing before a group of people. Then she announced that she might be ready to participate in a group workshop.

Facilitating workshops is another way that I serve Mother Earth and work for Dream Change Coalition. I have held workshops with one person and with five hundred people, in the United States, South America, Africa, and India. They have been held at established workshop centers such as The Omega Institute, at people's homes, and in rented halls. I have worked alone, co-facilitated with other workshop facilitators such as John Perkins, Ipupiara, Cleicha, Lyn Roberts-Herrick, and Mary Tendall, or been assisted by incredibly powerful teachers such as Robert Levy and Wendi Whitsett. Each workshop is unique; each circle has its own purpose and personality.

People come to my workshops from all professions and walks of life—shamanic practitioners and energy healers as well as people with no experience or knowledge of alternative healing techniques and philosophies. Physicians, dentists, nurses, housewives, teachers, astronomers, exotic dancers, writers, massage therapists, singers, artists—all are welcome, and all contribute in special ways to the experience of each and every one of us.

In the workshop Grace had joined, we sat in a circle around the altar where we had placed representations of the elements fire, water, earth, and air, along with huacas with which each of us had a deep personal relationship. All week we had been working together, clarifying our dreams, connecting with our guides and with the power of elemental forces, firming our intent, and breaking down barriers. We had become a tribe, and our dreams became one in the circle, interconnected with one another and with all our relations, human and other, now and forever. I told the group that tonight we would meet in ceremony, circled together by the fire, naked.

Grace gasped. She had bravely joined the circle all week, an act of enormous courage for someone who just recently had been afraid to leave her house. Slowly she had opened up to the group about her dreams and her barriers. As the week progressed, she found that her pointed and clear insight was of great help to many of us. She had become an integral member of the tribe that was our workshop circle. But meet naked?

"You're kidding," she exclaimed softly.

I looked her way, and my assistant moved to her side.

"You're not, I take it."

"No, Grace, I am not," I replied gently. "Those of you who look forward to the fire ceremony need not come unless you wish to support the others because you are already comfortable inhabiting your physical bodies in a communal context. Those of you who are uncomfortable with the thought, who feel it is something that you simply cannot do, will find—if you are able to push past that barrier—that this ceremony, in which we embody our spirits as a tribe, will be one of the most healing experiences of your life."

I was not sure that she would come. I don't think she was sure either.

That night we gathered by the lake to perform the ceremony. We removed our clothes and *camayed* (shared spirit with) one another by blowing a fine mist of water onto each other's bodies. Afterward, glowing wet in the light and warmth of the fire, we looked around as if seeing each other for the first time. Such a variety of shapes, ages, and sizes—each one perfectly divine.

After the ceremony I walked back toward my room. Hearing music, voices, and laughter, I entered a building where people had congregated to listen to music and dance. There in the middle of the floor was Grace. Fully clothed now, but wet and glowing with water, wine, and passion, she danced the night away, laughing, talking, and singing—a full member of the tribe. What a shapeshift! I smiled happily and joined in.

In the following pages I invite you to join me in a journey—the journey of my life—that led me to become both a surgeon and a shaman. This journey makes an interesting story, and I will share much of it with you if you decide to join me. But even more interesting is the nature of real change in anybody's life. What gives us the power to heal, grow, move in new directions, and embrace our true spirits—to shapeshift? My role as shaman and my role as surgeon are really one and the same role. In both capacities I am simply an agent of change. I stand ready to help people through the transformative gateways of their lives, but I personally cannot change anyone from the outside. The readiness for real change must come from within. The truly fascinating subject of this book is the capacity of each person to connect with the inner resources that allow that person to flower and live in ecstasy.

1
Looking Outside the Box

IT IS NIGHT and I sit here alone. I am alone with my self, the finite me that was born and will die. I sit alone, surrounded by things, objects that belong to the me that is. I sit here alone with my memories, thoughts, and feelings—the story that is me, that is this life.

I sit here alone like a grand oak tree, an oak tree alone in a field, surrounded by grasses, saplings, and flowers, crawling with insects, a home to fungi and moss. The tree is nourished by the water table, cleansed by the rain, breathing the air and the energy of the far-off star that is our sun, exchanging molecules with Mother Earth, changing through this communion moment by moment. Connected to the sky, the stars, and the planet, the tree is alone with its memories of its life, its own story etched into its bark and the rings of its trunk, in the shape and direction of its branches. The tree is its story, is formed by its memories. Is the tree lonely in its sense of self, in its being a tree that was born and that will die?

I sit here alone, a being that was born and that will die, shaped by my story, connected and communing with all that is, all that ever was, and all that ever will be.

I sit here alone and write that story, that reality that is my life.

The Reality Box

Reality. What is it? Is it fixed? From a very early age I grew up understanding that reality is not fixed or finite but is defined by the box that is our experience of the world. I was further led to understand that this box that is our notion of reality expands, contracts, and shifts with the events in our lives and the choices we make. We are all aware of times in our personal lives when we come to understand new distinctions, or of times in history when as a culture we see things that we were unaware of before.

It was my father, Marvin Weinstein, Ph.D., who taught me these concepts. Marvin was an only child who grew into a gentle, quiet genius. Accomplished at the clarinet and headed for a career in the symphony orchestra, he found himself in the U.S. Army at the onset of World War II. Over the next several years of his life, it seemed as though every obstacle he encountered turned into an opportunity. The army needed people who were versed in radar technology, and, seeing his aptitude, they sent him to what is now Case Western Reserve to study physics and electrical engineering. It was there that he became fascinated with relativity and quantum theory. Those were exciting times for everyone in the field of physics. My father was especially interested in the paradox that many concepts entirely adequate in one domain of experience—in fact, so familiar that they are the basis for common sense—are entirely inadequate and even wrong outside of that domain, such as the impact of motion at the speed of light upon time and space intervals described by the theory of relativity. Two weeks after D-day, he found himself discharged from the army for poor eyesight, free to move to the West Coast, where he enrolled at the University of California, Berkeley, to study physics, first with David Bohm in late 1944, and later with Robert Oppenheimer.

There he met my mother, Fay Byron, who was herself a graduate student in physics. Soon afterward, she decided that she wanted to be a doctor. Just around the time that she was accepted into medical school at Temple University in Philadelphia, Oppenheimer became the director of the Institute for Advanced Study at Princeton. My father, having obtained his master's degree and having published the results of research conducted under Oppenheimer's guidance, arranged to switch to Princeton University to complete his Ph.D. in theoretical physics—and, very fortunately, to be near my mother. They lived together in Philadelphia, my father commuting almost daily to Princeton. Bohm was also teaching at Princeton and became my father's thesis advisor. In addition, my father worked as Bohm's research assistant, his main job being that of assisting in the writing of Bohm's famous book on quantum theory.

The war took its toll on the key players in the field of physics; Bohm was suspended from Princeton for a year after being subpoenaed to be questioned by the House Un-American Activities Committee. He spent the year visiting Einstein on a daily basis, returning to discuss many of Einstein's theories and concepts with my father. It was during this year that Bohm began to seriously question some of the existing interpretations of quantum theory, and to develop what is now referred to as Bohmian mechanics. In 1951, rather than appear before the House Un-American Activities Committee, Bohm left the country for good, going first to the University of São Paulo in Brazil.

My father had not yet finished his Ph.D. research, and he accepted a position as a lecturer in atomic physics and a fellowship in biophysics at the Johnson Foundation of the University of Pennsylvania in Philadelphia. My mother graduated from Temple in 1951 and began her internship at Mt. Zion hospital in San Francisco. My father joined her there, still not having completed his Ph.D., and went to work for Pacific Gas and Electric. At this time Bohm began writing to ask my father to join him in São Paulo. My parents then found themselves in the position of choosing between leaving the United States so that my father's partnership and work with Bohm could continue or staying in the land where their respective families lived, and where my mother could begin her planned residency at the Cleveland Clinic.

Throughout my childhood I heard tales of my parents' early life together. My father shared his wonder at how obstacles turned into opportunities, and how he learned to explore the myriad possibilities of discovery that the universe held. He taught me that if we hold on to the need to explain everything that we see and experience, we cannot see or experience anything outside of the box of what we already know. Then we will not make any authentic progress in enhancing our understanding of the world.

The Box Blows Wide Apart

Many years later—the mid 1990s—I experienced an event that forced me to expand the box that had been my reality. It all started with a backache.

"Ouch, that hurts!" I was facedown on the table as Paula, a chiropractor, adjusted my back. As she worked she chatted, "I'm going to Ecuador in a few months." "How wonderful!" I replied grumpily and without conviction.

My back had given out and I was in extreme pain. I could barely walk. With a busy surgical schedule ahead of me, I needed to get well fast! Disappointed in the ability of Western doctors—M.D.s—to effectively treat back pain, I sought out Paula. After the session she handed me some information about her upcoming trip. Rushing out to my car to get back to work, I threw the papers in the back.

The week wore on, and my back improved. Pain free, I returned to the operating room and regained my effectiveness, my health, and my disposition. Cleaning out my car on the weekend, I came across the printed material.

> From Incas to headshrinkers, a high adventure for those who truly want to learn and to help educate others, who believe that—as the shamans say—"the world is as you dream it," and that each of us has the ability to create beauty and influence humanity's future relationship with nature. Come with Dream Change Coalition on a transformational trip to the Andes and Amazon to witness and experience ancient healing techniques handed down through the millennia and still used today. Visit indigenous communities living connected to the earth and spirit in ecstatic ways and recapture the ecstasy of your own life.

Sounds fascinating, I thought. *Recapture the ecstasy in life. Is that possible for me?* For some reason I felt drawn. Compelled to pursue this journey, I was strangely not compelled to discover the reason behind my compulsion. When I called the toll-free number, a voice from the travel agency came on, announcing that the trip was full. The agent put me on the waiting list.

Then, a few weeks before the departure date, Paula broke her ankle. She stayed in Baltimore; I went to Ecuador. Paula did make the trip three months later, where she met another Dream Change trip participant, the man who is now her husband and the father of her daughter.

The trip that I went on was unusual in that the majority of the participants lived within the Washington, D.C./Baltimore corridor. For about three months—even before the travel agency notified me that there was a space for me—I attended the monthly gatherings held by the trip co-facilitator, Joyce Ferranti, to help the travelers prepare and get to know one another. Our group included psychotherapists, nurses, massage therapists, dentists, and other health care professionals. We met monthly with Joyce and a Brazilian shaman, Ipupiara. At first the meetings were awkward and, for many of us, brought up familiar doubts about our choices. Who are these people? What am I doing—going on a trip to a strange place with a bunch of strange people to meet with strange shamans? Such doubts, reflecting our personal levels of comfort and discomfort, are the blocks or walls we all encounter during any transformative process. If we manage to break through them, we can expand our horizons, open to new worlds of possibility, and find much deeper levels of comfort.

Each month we would sit together in a circle and discuss our dreams, our fears, our intentions. Ipupiara would then drum and chant, leading us on journeys. After a couple of meetings, none of this seemed strange. Our group of strangers began to bond as a supportive tribe, ready for anything, and excited about the possibilities of our personal and communal transformation. Shaman Ipupiara is of the Urue-wau-wau people, a tribe that was almost completely decimated by the devastation of the Brazilian rainforest. At the time of our meetings there were about eighty-five tribe members left in existence; now there are only about forty. He spoke of his people, of the indigenous wisdom of the forest, and of healing. As we started to explore the lives and dreams of the people that we would soon visit, the lives and dreams of the forest and its inhabitants, we also began to revisit and reassess the dream of our industrialized society.

Our ancestors had a good dream of security, opportunity, comfort, and leisure time for their descendants, but this dream was lost in the means they used to manifest it. The dream became one of consumption, construction, and conquest. The dream became one of a world of imperialism—of men over women, of whites over all other races, of haves over have-nots, of complexity over simplicity, of specialization and separate pieces over the united whole. It became a dream of domination of the mind over the heart, and of humans over all our relations—other humans, the animals, the rivers, the rocks, the air—all our relations. In this process we had become a community separated from the earth, from spirit, and from each other. But now we were learning about a different way of seeing reality, and our anticipation of the trip was growing.

Excitement abounded when the day finally came for us to fly to the Miami airport to meet John Perkins and the travelers who were coming from other cities. But as I fastened my seat belt, the familiar doubts returned: *Why am I doing this?* When I ask people on the Dream Change trips I now facilitate why they are coming with me, I frequently hear the echo of my answer at that time: "I don't know." Indeed, I had no conscious idea why I was going. It was not a good time in my life. I didn't really have the finances or time to go, and I was going through extreme relationship problems. Although outwardly I was a huge success, on the inside I was crumbling.

The outside: a large successful practice in cosmetic surgery; four terrific children and a granddaughter; two dogs, two cats; a beautiful home—the Great American Dream! I had made it! Right?

The inside: My world as I knew it had collapsed. My family was literally falling to pieces. I had separated from my husband of over twenty years just weeks before. I was alone with four children and a mountain of debt. I had a life that kept me prisoner to the banks holding my loans. I was engulfed by conflicting feelings: pain, anger, sorrow, sadness, relief, joy, hope. Emotions swirled around a numb core as I moved through each day like a zombie without any idea what the next step would or could be.

I was at the pinnacle of a dream, and looking at my success, I had to face the fact that much of it was my husband's dream, and that we were no longer dreaming together. Our dream together was dead. I was experiencing painfully and at first hand the consequences of losing clarity about one's own dream in life. And I now faced those consequences ahead of me. I would pay in many ways: custody and child support battles with lawyers; psychotherapy for me and my children; isolation; tears and more tears.

Suffering. Chaos. Change. We all go through periods of chaos and change in our lives. Looking back later in life, we can even see the benefit that came of these changes. Then why the suffering? Is it possible that we can learn to trust that there is opportunity within the chaos? Can we flow through change with less suffering and more grace? Can we let ourselves feel our feelings—without the overlay of thoughts and judgements—and then release them?

These are all good questions, and yet it is difficult to see things this way in the midst of a storm like the one that surrounded me as I sat on the plane and asked myself why. Why on earth was I going to Ecuador? Shouldn't I be at home trying to hold on to what was left of my life as I knew it? Shouldn't I be trying to stem the tide of change coursing through my life? All these "shouldn'ts" didn't seem to hold the weight that they might have in the past. I simply knew that I had to go. I was drawn. Fate? Kismet? The grand forces of nature? Call it what you will, I was on my way to Ecuador.

The day before departure, I had started to feel ill while packing. At first I thought it was fatigue combined with excitement. But as the day wore on, I had to admit that I felt terrible! My nose was running; my sinuses were heavy. I had gone to the pharmacy for medication and took it, eager to recover for the trip, but slept only fitfully. On the flight to Miami and then on to Quito, I kept getting worse and worse.

In Quito we were met by Dream Change's Ecuadorian partner, Juan Gabriel Carrasco, with a bus on which we would travel throughout the country. We filed onto the bus to take our seats and started out of the city.

"Joyce," I cried, "I need a plastic bag fast!" She laughed, but the look on my face quickly persuaded her that I was not joking. I began to vomit, and my fever rose to an alarming extent. For the next two days, bent over a series of plastic bags, I vomited such large volumes that by the time we reached our first destination, the home of the shaman Alberto Tatzo, I was dehydrated, feverish, and so weak that I had to be carried to a bed to lie down. Alone, I continued to throw up and began to cry.

The rest of the group gathered to meet with Alberto Tatzo. Don Alberto is often called "the Jesus of the Andes," both for his physical appearance and for his teaching ways: his eloquent speeches; his strong, beautiful, and pure philosophies; and his kind, gentle nature. I was oblivious to all of this as I lay in bed. I don't know how long I lay there, but I remember sitting up in bed just as someone came in. It was John Perkins.

Somehow I had known before he arrived that it was time. I grabbed the blanket around me and prepared to go to don Alberto even before John could say that he thought I should go. He led me to join the rest of the group in the circular room with the fire pit in the middle, the room where the shaman taught and performed his healing ceremonies.

We were high in the Andes and the night air was chilly, yet I was burning up with fever. I lay with my hot cheek against the cold brick floor. There were books and blackboards around the edges of the room and branches, herbs, stones, and water by the fire burning in the center—but I took in none of this at the time. I only knew that I needed help, and I somehow knew that the shaman was the one to help me.

After a time he began his healings. "Who wants to be first?" I heard Juan translate to the group. Despite my illness, my hand flew up with such determination that I astounded myself. I seemed to be led by an inner self that knew what I needed. I remember a strange sense of calm knowing, of familiarity, of being home. The ceremony utilized the four elements—fire, water, earth, and air—and was conducted with branches, herbs, feathers, and stones that had been gathered to move "energy."

Too weak to stand before the shaman, I sat on the dirt floor by the fire, holding on to the rocks at the edge of the circle for support. Chanting melodically, don Alberto rhythmically brushed me with aromatic branches, shared spirit with me by spraying me with a fine mist of herbal water, surrounded me with smoke and incense, and cleansed my aura with flapping feathers.

Nothing was ingested, nothing was physically or chemically manipulated. In no way did the healing resemble any technique that I had been taught in medical school. Nothing in my life to date had prepared me for this, yet I held no fear or doubt, only calm assurance. The healing took about half an hour. During that time I felt my strength return, the nausea abate, and my spirits build in ecstasy. Afterward I stood and thanked don Alberto. He hugged me and said how happy he was to see me again. I had never been to Ecuador nor met him in this life, yet I knew him at a very deep soul level. We had been together in the past. I can barely find the words to describe what I felt. I had no context in which to place this experience.

But it had happened. That I could not deny, and I could never go back. I had experienced something that challenged everything that I had studied so long and hard to know about health and the human body. I had stepped outside the box that had been my reality up until then, and I was seeing with new eyes. I had come to the interface between two realities, two ways of viewing the universe. I thought of my father and recognized the opportunity that was opening up before me—an opportunity to expand the box that is our reality, that is our knowledge of health and healing.

What happened after that? The next morning don Alberto held a dawn ceremony to salute Inti, the sun, and a water ceremony at his community's sacred springs. I hiked to the ceremonial sites along with the rest of the group. We then drove down the Pastaza River canyon, flew into the Amazon jungle, hiked to the thermal falls . . . in short, I carried on with the trip through the Andes and the Amazon basin with the rest of the group, meeting with numerous other shamans. I was well. I was healed. I was able to participate fully in the entire magical and transformational journey!

It was almost a year later when the severity of my illness hit me. "Weren't you worried?" I asked John. "What were you going to do about me if the healing didn't work?" He admitted that he had decided to send me back to Quito the next morning so that the rest of the group could carry on with the rigorous trip into the jungle unhindered. Then he added, "But somehow I knew that wasn't going to be necessary. That's why I came to get you that night—to bring you into the room for a healing."

Somehow we both knew. Looking back on that night, I am struck with many questions. I am a physician, a surgeon, with board certification in both general and plastic surgery. I had trained for many, many years to become a plastic surgeon—four years of medical school, five years of general surgery residency, two years of plastic surgery residency. I had no previous experience with non-allopathic healing techniques. Why was I not demanding to get to a phone? To be taken to a doctor or the nearest hospital? To be given medicine? To get back to Quito? To return to the States?

That night I was led by an inner knowing. Perhaps my whole life had led me to that night. In half an hour with Alberto Tatzo, I was introduced to a whole new world—a new way of looking at health, at life, at healing. It in no way fit into the box of what I knew and had studied so long and hard to know. It in no way fit into my model of the body or of scientific method. I could not explain. And that night I let go of the need to explain.

My father had taught me well. Even in our culture, every great scientist knows that the true quantum leaps in understanding come only after letting go of the need to explain. One thousand years ago we "knew" that the sun revolved around the earth. Five hundred years ago we "knew" that the world was flat. One hundred years ago we "knew" that time was linear and absolute. Today we "know" that healing occurs through anatomical and biochemical manipulations. We "know" that there is separation between body and spirit. We "know" that if something does not fit into a proof by standard scientific method, it doesn't exist.

What will we "know" tomorrow?

Do we believe what we see, or see what we believe?

2

The Dream Called Doctor

MY FRIEND SHRUTHI SIGHED DEEPLY as we relaxed in her dorm room at Harvard in Boston. "Medical school is taking its toll on me. Overall, it's not that it's intellectually challenging. It's more memorization and application than it is developing new concepts. But it is tough. At times I wonder if I'm in the right place. I feel pulled in two, wondering if I am doing the right thing. How can I treat people as a whole with the training that I am getting, which stresses the minutiae? What is holistic medicine anyway? The more I learn, the less I feel sure of." She was just beginning her training at Harvard Medical School, after having studied shamanic ways of healing. "Do you feel the same way about being a doctor as you did when you started?" she asked me. Though I had completed my training many years before, her question made me recall how I had felt as a beginning, fresh student. I had been eager to learn and to be of service in the fight against disease. What had happened to that feeling? And what had first led me to choose that path, to dream that dream?

My mother was also a physician. She always cautioned me against medicine as a career, warning me about the interference of the medical bureaucracy and the personal cost of trying to manifest the ideal of being a true healer of people. However, when I first told her that I had decided to apply to medical school, she admitted to how pleased she was—pleased that I would be her colleague, that I would understand her language when she talked in medical terms, and that I would understand who she is and what she went through. She reassured me that much nobility remained in the field of medicine, despite the troubles in the profession.

I had chosen to embark on the dream of becoming a doctor. I dreamed of learning to heal people; I dreamed of learning to heal my own emotional wounds; and I dreamed of being a good caretaker for my children.

"So much has transpired since I first began medical school," I told Shruthi.

"Tell me about your first semester," she urged.

"I can smell it to this day! I remember it well," I replied. We had been in medical school five weeks. Formalin had penetrated so deeply into our skin and soft tissues that, no matter how much we showered or washed, the smell remained a part of us. Or perhaps it was simply embedded into our memories . . . and still is.

"Good morning, hun! How is Maude today? Did you sleep?" Our group had a female cadaver, donated by the wish of the dying woman, well preserved and with a thick layer of subcutaneous fat. Other cadavers were the unclaimed dead of the city, wan and thin. Even in death they held themselves with an air of loneliness and of desperation.

As I walked around the room I took in the rows of tables, covers from the night removed, the partially dissected bodies lined up in ghoulish queues. There was a cigar in one mouth, a tie around a neck, a hat on another. We had given names to our cadavers and made feeble attempts to kid each other about their stories, their former positions, their lives, their families. But it was only ourselves we were kidding, using humor to ease the painful passage.

With lofty ideals, we had embarked on the long path leading to the profession and identity of doctor. Now, with our undergraduate studies and testing behind us, the fabric of our next decade was slowly sinking in. Already sleep deprived, we had begun the process—known as medical school—of being molded into the Western doctor.

This was the first rite of passage. It was the beginning of the systematic process that would isolate us and distance us from our patients. Our patients would become a diffuse "them," defined as sets of disease patterns and characteristics, without consideration of their lives, their hopes, their loves. We were taught that this distance is absolutely necessary, and that we would need to learn to be "objective." We were taught that it is impossible to treat patients without objectivity. That is why we were told that it is unwise to treat members of our own families or other loved ones.

When did this cultural belief system, this absolute "truth," begin? The old family doctor certainly didn't always follow these rules. In my grandmother's time the family doctor was often the only physician around. Distance from his patients' lives and problems was not an option. Everyone he knew was his patient.

I certainly didn't learn it from my mother. Fay, a board-certified pathologist, has been one of my greatest teachers. When I was in my second year of medical school, she wrote to me:

Dearest Evie:

I am moved to write a letter to my daughter the doctor. . . . I pray you be spared any temptation to any protection from the dazzling and dangerous universe. Accept contradiction, insecurity, change, and the unknown as your condition of life; learn to love the fact that there are as many brilliant aspects of reality as stars in the Milky Way. The lucky man or woman "sails the soul" without a guide in the winds of time and chance and space. For him or her, instead of certitude, there is endless wonder.

As to medicine—if you are too proud to assume when necessary the silly self-righteous attitudes of your club, at least nominally in support of guild dogma, you will be behaving as a rigid idiot. You cannot unify a perception that is intellectual and innovative with the standards of pompous righteousness that the vast majority of your colleagues feel comfortable with. Fake it, my love, and do it winsomely.

You must learn to be many things to many people. You must develop the ability to think, act, and perceive on several levels and not pig-headedly expect to find or give consistency—that way lies madness. Doctors who insist on living all their life in one character end up as suicides. Patients also require a quick shifting of postures and roles to find one that fits.

You will be heir to many blessings as a physician; you will be able to
know and render help to your family, children, and friends that you could
never give unless you were a physician—and one who stays informed in
general areas of medical care.
    Aloha,
    Mama

She taught me through her wise words and through her example. Long
a proponent of integrating "folk" medicines, she would more often than not
incorporate foods, baths, and teas into her prescriptions. To her a hot bath
could help cure virtually anything.

Heir to Many Blessings

My mother was born in the mountains of Colorado in a sod house. Half of
her family of poor Irish immigrants were placard-waving atheists, a fiery
people with beliefs as firm as any fundamentalist. They were known as the
stone throwers of County Cork. The other half, devout Catholics, prayed
tirelessly for the souls of their kin. After the early death of my grandfather
and uncle, the women of my maternal family struggled to survive. Grandmother Winifred was a schoolteacher.

As a child I loved to hear the stories of my mother's and aunts' lives. I
asked my mother over and over again to recount the stories of her childhood—of the wild burros that would carry them over the deep canyons of
Colorado, walking on the thin water pipes that connected the heights; of
the time when my grandmother was a teacher on a reservation in the Southwest; and of the valley of rattlesnakes where their indigenous friends would
lead them to play with the serpents. I was thrilled by my mother's stories of
herself as a young woman, jumping freight trains with the hobos, riding the
country free and wild.

Life was hard for her. She worked for wages from a very early age,
earning money any way she could to help her family. It was feast or famine
in her early life. Even many years later, when our family could afford any-

thing we wanted, she still took special pleasure in creating a great feast to eat—turkey with all the fixings, apple pie fragrant with cinnamon, and home-baked bread. She had a saying: "Eat for the hunger that's coming."

There is no question that her childhood was challenging, and yet perhaps this was indeed a gift. Perhaps it was this very struggle that gave her the tools to elevate everyone around her in a way that savored all of life, that remained true to her core values, that recognized the fervor of human honor and of nature.

Against great odds, she graduated from Temple Medical School, class of 1951. After being accepted into medical school, she had gone for her admissions meeting, knowing that she had no money for her tuition. She laughed at the admissions officer when he asked her how she was going to pay. Taking her laughter as a sign of carefree high social standing, he dropped the question and she began classes. Later she won a full scholarship, enabling her to complete her training. Few women attempted the rigorous regime of medical school in those days; she was one of only a dozen women in her class of several hundred. The pressure was so severe that one of her fellow students—a dear friend—broke under it and was institutionalized. My mother told me that when she began medical school, the dean called all the women together and said to them, "I call you here to tell you that we don't want you here. The reason that you are here is that some of our contributors insisted that we have a small percentage of women. But remember, you are not wanted!"

After medical school she began a residency in internal medicine at the Cleveland Clinic. After one year she stopped her residency for the birth of my brother Joseph, and she opened a private practice as a general practitioner. Her office was in the city above a Chinese laundry, and she developed a large practice, mostly of indigent people. Treating the poor and destitute on a daily basis, she was drained by the dramas and the sorrows of her patients' lives. Burned out from private practice, she returned to training, this time a residency in pathology, where she achieved board certification with the American Board of Pathologists.

Mother endured backbreaking work schedules and soul-breaking expectations. Her training was difficult, and her post-residency work in the hospitals was even worse. Her honesty often got her into a great deal of trouble with hospital administrators. She bemoaned the fact that those in the administration were forever concerned with how the autopsies read, frequently objecting to her diagnoses and choice of words. Yet she persevered, standing up for patients' rights and refusing to change the documents despite severe consequences. She had not yet learned to support the "guild dogma" that she wrote to me about many years later. She stayed the course, and she suffered the consequences, resulting in her later choosing to leave the country that she and her family had called home.

From her, I learned to endure. "You get used to hanging if you hang long enough," she would often say. I also learned grace, and to revere life and all its glories, even at times of extreme hardship. At the most trying of times, she would find beauty in the world about her: in places, animals, and plants; in food, aromas, and textures; in the hearts and words of people; in literature, art, and music.

Passionate about the beauty of life, she and my father cultivated orchids, other ornamental plants, and rare fruit trees. They used to spout the Latin names of plants and trees as they took us for walks in the woods and through botanical gardens. The world of nature was our temple and cathedral where they taught us to revere and connect with everything around us.

Looking back at her life, I see that my mother faced and conquered innumerable challenges, learning to maintain a focused vision of her values and the essence of her dreams. She acted with determination and took total responsibility for putting her dreams into action. A passionate activist, she believed in the importance of all humanity and the validity of each person's contribution to society. A card-carrying Communist in her college days, she denounced oppression everywhere. Later, denouncing oppression in Russia, she left the Communist party. She was an activist in the civil rights and anti-war movements. Many of my early memories were of her at protest marches, never backing down, even to the point of being arrested and detained. Fiery and passionate, she taught me to continually assess and reassess my beliefs and stands and to take action for the higher good of all.

After our family had moved to Kenya, she ran the laboratory at the hospital in Nakuru. There she developed a system something like a socialist community. The disparity in salaries was obscenely unfair to her mind, the native Africans being compensated with far less than Europeans at the same skill level. She set up a procedure outside of the governmentally run organization. Each person in the enterprise had a number of shares, based on his or her skill level, from the lab technicians right down to housekeeping. The number of shares for each person was determined and voted upon by all. Contributing her own salary and any income from work in the private sector, my mother divided up the earnings among all participants, based upon their number of shares, at the end of each month.

In her later years she had a private practice in Hawaii, where her patients consisted of a large population of indigenous Hawaiians, as well as peoples from throughout Oceania and the Far East. Many of her patients would go between her and indigenous healers—kahunas and others—a practice she encouraged and honored. Sometimes I couldn't figure out who gave more advice about health and living, my mother or her patients. The entire family's ideas were taken into account. Every health problem that came up was discussed, all opinions were considered as options for treatment. Everyone involved had input into the treatment plan. It would seem that she never caught on to the idea of distancing. She was a true scientist with a keen intellect, yet she was always involved with her patients, their lives, their achievements, and their follies. She loved them and they loved her. I recall my mother's patients bringing her gifts—deep sea divers with huge trees of black coral, mothers carrying enormous trays of food and inviting us to their daughters' weddings.

The Illusion of Separation

Early on in the course of my medical training I remember my mother telling me, "Always listen to your patients. They are telling you their diagnosis in their own words. Many doctors forget to listen. The patient will tell you everything you need to know." In medical school, when we came to study physical diagnosis, this concept was reiterated by my teachers. "Over ninety percent of diagnoses are made by listening to the patient's history alone," they taught. "The physical examination and laboratory tests serve only to confirm what is found through taking the history." I excelled at listening. I aced physical diagnosis.

I failed at distancing.

There we were in the waiting area of the emergency room, arms around each other, both sobbing. Someone ran for tissues. Recalling the incident, I can't even remember her name. Or her son's. Yet the memory still brings salty tears to my eyes.

I was the surgical resident on call that night in Baltimore's Saint Agnes Hospital emergency room. Responsible for all surgical emergencies, I had been called when a victim of a shooting accident was brought in. I was well versed in trauma resuscitation and surgery, having been trained at the world-renowned Shock Trauma Institute, also of Baltimore. But Saint Agnes was not a trauma center, and when a major accident victim was triaged there, it was because the person was pretty much doomed—too unstable to survive the helicopter ride downtown.

He was twelve, the age of my son Michael. The medics rushed in, moving him onto a treatment room stretcher while rapidly shouting out what information they had garnered at the scene. His father was a police officer. He and his brother had been playing with their father's gun. The kids hadn't realized that it was loaded.

The boy was holding his intestines in his hands, a look of terror on his face. Blood poured onto the stretcher, my hands, my clothes, the floor. Racing around in calm panic, barking orders to nurses, lower residents, and assistants, I commenced the resuscitation procedures. We worked on him frantically, using every trick in the book, as the life flooded out of his little body.

It was my job to go out to the waiting room and tell his mother. *I'm sorry . . . we did all we could. We put up a good fight, but. . . . He's out of pain now. . . .* I practiced possible phrases in my mind, discarding them one by one as too trite, too insubstantial, too inadequate. In the end, we held each other and cried.

"Maintain a professional distance." That is what we had been taught. "Don't get personally involved." Not becoming personally involved was one thing; not being a person was another.

The distancing had begun in the anatomy lab in medical school. While we trained in the hospitals on clinical rotations, distancing was experientially practiced. Perhaps the most difficult field in which to practice distancing was psychiatry, the field of the mind and of the emotions. And yet this was the field more than any other where the teachers stressed the importance of remaining uninvolved with the patients. "Be a blank slate," we heard over and over. "Just listen. Don't react. Don't become involved."

On my psychiatry rotation I was assigned to a man who came to the clinic. Very quickly it became apparent that he was a homicidal paranoid. Each week he would recount more and more atrocities he had executed; how he had maimed and tortured his cousin, his neighbor, strangers. Each week I would try to be blank, a blank slate. I would try just to listen and not react. Don't react? Are you kidding me? I was terrified each and every day! I received praise and high marks for the way in which I was able to make this guarded, paranoid individual open up to me. I was praised for my interviewing skills. I wasn't sure who was more crazy, the patient or the doctors.

As we studied, we learned the language of medicine, a language with which doctors communicate to other doctors and health care workers. I later realized that the words we use as doctors hold meanings for us as we communicate to one another in a non-emotional, uninvolved manner, that are very different from the meanings they convey to our patients and their families. Little did we know that the training we were getting was setting the stage for miscommunication with our patients later. For how can you communicate when you speak different languages?

Our language was changing in many ways. On our ward rotations we referred to the patients with peculiar names—"the femur" or "the radius" in orthopedics; "the gallbladder" or "the hernia" in general surgery; "the diabetic" or "the M.I." in internal medicine. To me the patients were Mrs. Romanowski, Mr. Weber, little Karen. They had real names, faces, fears, passions, hopes, prayers, lives, and families. I excelled at interviewing skills.

And I failed at blank slate.

Communing and communicating with these patients and their families on the wards, I noticed their frustration, and I became frustrated. Aside from a few acute episodes of infectious disease, I never saw a single patient cured of his or her disease. Diseases were managed, yes. Cured . . . not really.

Disillusioned with the practice of medicine, I turned to surgery. Although detachment was still expected, the surgeons had much more fun. We joked with our patients and with the staff. There were times of overwhelming adrenaline rushes and excitement, raw energy, and power. Times of pure fear, rapid diagnosis, rapid decision making, rapid action. We were charged, and discharged, regularly. And we could see ourselves actually helping people.

In other fields of medicine it felt as though we were simply managing diseases, keeping them at bay, minimizing symptoms, cajoling our patients to do as we advised. We managed people's diabetes, their arthritis, their hypertension, even their cancers. We sometimes saw cancers go away, only to later see a reoccurrence or a second primary source for cancer.

In surgery it was said that we "healed with steel." If someone appeared to have acute appendicitis, we made a diagnosis, went into the operating room, and immediately found out if we were right or wrong. Our diagnostic acumen was continually tested, and we honed our diagnostic and technical skills quickly. Instant diagnosis, instant gratification. Appendix inflamed? Go into the operating room and take it out. They came in sick. They left well.

Looking back on it all, I wonder whether it was a cop-out on my part. I couldn't find it in me to just manage diseases, to become detached and to admonish my patients, to tell them day in and day out what is "right" and "wrong" for them. Did we truly know what was "right" for anyone else, and if so, then why was it so hard to get people to listen? I couldn't do what the institution of medicine asked of me, so I turned to a field where I would have minimal contact with the patients. In surgery there was rapid turnover. Patients were in and out of the hospital, and they were under anesthesia most of the time I was with them, anyway. I didn't have to grapple with my feelings about the inadequacies of our profession—were we helping people live better lives, or were we prolonging death?

Later I took another step in this direction. I turned to plastic surgery. People come in desiring an external change, and it is done. Quick, straightforward, fun. Right? Yet something was missing here, too. In plastic surgery residency we were told that some patients come in because they want a new relationship or a better relationship, a better job, a better life. *Some* patients? Try all patients. Who doesn't want that? Whether the individual patient focuses on his nose, her breasts, or elsewhere, they all want to change their lives in some way. We were told that we had to be sure to specify that we as surgeons could not deliver a change in their lives.

They came in asking me for a change, a change in their bodies. After delivering this change, I discovered that some patients were not happy with the results of plastic surgery, no matter how good a job I had done.

Ann was a successful and wealthy businesswoman. Married to a younger man, her second husband, she came to me interested in rejuvenation surgery, a facelift. We had several consultations before we decided on the exact procedures. In our numerous meetings I came to know her well. She was filled with a bitter anger about her life, her relationships, her future. Never smiling, she looked older than her age of 48. After four lengthy consultations she elected to have a facelift and a forehead lift, upper and lower eyelid surgery, and a fat graft into her lips to make them more youthful and full. It took ten hours in the operating room. She healed well and without difficulties. In her follow-up over the next year, I watched her progress. In pictures, she looked different, younger. Her pre- and postoperative photos revealed a remarkable change in her appearance. Yet in person I saw the same angry, bitter, unhappy woman. On the rare occasions that she smiled, she even looked pretty and approachable. But for her, the major external change was not accompanied by an internal change. In person she did not give the impression of either youth or beauty, despite the fine features. She was very unhappy with her change. Her life was the same as it had been before her surgery, or worse. She asked for more surgery. She became increasingly angry as she searched for someone outside herself who could give her a satisfactory solution to her problematic situation in life, a solution that she was sure she deserved.

I learned painfully that I, indeed, could not deliver change unless my patients were ready, but over time I came to realize that the patients themselves could. They can and do change.

Tilly came to my office with her mother. She sat with her head bowed, looking down at her hands through the entire consultation, never volunteering anything, speaking only when spoken to. Her mother did the talking for her. Her daughter wanted a breast augmentation, implants. She had never developed in the chest and wore a AA brassiere. She had been asking for this surgery for a long time. I examined her, then spoke to her and her mother about her options. Through the hour-long consultation I came to know her as shy and withdrawn, unsure of herself, without voice, without passion.

She was, however, very knowledgeable and had a keen intellect. She was serious about her studies as a nursing student and was at the top of her class. But she wasn't sure which field of nursing she should pursue. They were all interesting, she told me, but she wasn't drawn to any particular type of nursing.

Tilly proceeded with implant surgery. Recovering well, she continued her studies. In the ensuing year, as she came back to my office for follow-up visits, I witnessed her changing in every way. She was hardly recognizable as the same young woman who had sat with her hands in her lap such a short time before. She soon stopped bringing her mother. She would sashay into the room, head uplifted, exuding confidence, glowing with inner beauty, charisma, sensuality, even sexual power. About six months after surgery she told me about her boyfriend—she was in love for the first time. After eight months she announced that although she had graduated from nursing school, she found no pleasure in being a nurse. She got a job as a graphic artist, something about which she spoke with passion and joy. To this day she is happy and accomplished in her new field.

Tilly had a minor physical change, yet she subsequently changed in all aspects—her internal and external beauty, her relationships, her job, her life—a true shapeshift!

I slowly came to realize that for true change to occur, external physical change has to be coupled with an internal change. Later, during my apprenticeship with shamans throughout the world, I came to understand that there is no separation between the internal and the external. Our internal beings—our emotional, mental, and spiritual bodies—are one with our physical body. The notion that the physical is somehow separate from the internal and spiritual is a long-held illusion. The resulting blocks exact personal and communal costs that are widespread in our culture, and astounding in their severity and diversity.

Who would have thought that a cosmetic plastic surgeon would become involved in shamanism and become dedicated to bringing forth indigenous wisdom, to bridging the worlds? Someone up there must have a considerable sense of humor! But if I had never been a practicing cosmetic surgeon, I might never have come to fully understand the degree of our disconnection, the depth of our sorrow, the extent of our woundedness as a culture, and our very real need to become reconnected, to be whole. Great spirit works in mysterious ways indeed!

3

Choose Your Dream—
Create Your World

MY FATHER'S EXAMPLE, which taught me to look outside the box, and my mother's refusal to accept the stance of professional distance in her doctor-patient relationships, set the stage for my own journey toward understanding the nature of real healing. I believe that in life there are no coincidences. Though I didn't know it at the time, my decision at age fifteen to carry an unplanned pregnancy to term would turn out to be pivotal to my understanding of how we create our own realities.

January 1965—Mombasa Harbor, Kenya

I was ten years of age. My brothers Benjamin and Joseph and I watched as the cargo was unloaded from the ship. We had arrived in Africa. The sweat poured down our dusty faces as we ran around waiting for the next leg of our journey to begin. Unfamiliar smells wafted through the African air, vendors selling peanuts and unripe mangoes sprinkled with cayenne. We watched as our parents made arrangements to drive inland to Nairobi, where we would discover Africa, land of primal beauty—stark, cruel, raw. In this ancient land of the sun and the shadow, life's vitality surged, yet was surrounded by death, circling like the vultures.

The duality of life—joyful creation and stark destruction—had been the constant teacher of my childhood. My father's parents were both Russian Jews from near Minsk who met in the United States. When my grandfather Michael was four years old, he was found in the pool of his own parents' blood after a pogrom ravaged through their village. He was adopted by the Weinsteins of Germany and later came to live in the United States, well away from the horrors of his childhood memories. Later, when Hitler came into power and tales of the atrocities toward his fellow Jews came to my grandfather's ears, he acted to help children caught in the web of similar nightmares by running an underground railroad for children of the concentration camps. As a child in Cleveland I remember playing with kids branded with telltale numeric tattoos on their arms.

In his own way my father fought against the horrors of the war through his work in physics. It was a time of excitement, pride, and purpose for physicists. As the horrors of Hitler's regime were revealed, they were driven to stop him at all costs. Later, the true costs became clear when the atom bombs were dropped. The heavy responsibility hit hard, and the field of nuclear physics fell from grace. My father was never the same, and he began to lose his passion for doing research in physics.

Through listening to him recount his experiences, I saw at a young age the necessity of clarifying goals and of keeping sight of the essence of your dream. I also saw the great price exacted when you lose track of your dream and put energy into a dream that has lost its essential clarity and core. I saw the price in my father's pain and anguish over the consequences of Hiroshima and Nagasaki.

After the war, the focus of his life became his marriage to my mother and caring for her four boys from her previous marriage and their three children together. My mother set up a family practice. My father decided to find work as far from the armaments field as possible, and he went to work as a consulting physicist for the General Electric lamp division. He completed his Ph.D. at Princeton and continued to work at GE for the next thirteen years, always interested in doing a good job, but without the passion he had felt for his earlier work. He became widely known among the small worldwide community of physicists doing research on the production of light, and some of his papers on the thermodynamics of radiation are still being cited, forty years after they were written. When my mother went on to study pathology and became disillusioned with the bureaucratic requirements for documentation without regard for what she considered truth, they reassessed the life that was their dream, for themselves and for their family.

For years my parents had discussed how difficult it is to think outside of the box that is one's own culture, and they decided as parents that the best thing they could do for their children would be to give them the opportunity to be a part of another culture for some years. In addition, my mother felt that practicing medicine in a so-called underprivileged country would be the most generous thing she could do as a doctor. After the assassination of President Kennedy, she and my father decided that it was time to leave the United States once and for all.

Broken, disillusioned, concerned about the influences of the distorted values of American life on their youngest children, my parents sold everything. They parted with so many beloved things—their orchids, their home, their books, their dreams. They would no longer live the American dream and imbue their children with wishes of "success," of the material world, of the illusions, of the life that to them had become a lie. Leaving the United States behind, they set off in search of a true significance in life, of meaning and values.

My parents had chosen. We packed up and drove. Our first destination was Mexico, an ancient land. There we found a home in the mountains and regrouped, enjoying a six-month respite before settling on a more permanent course of action, before clarifying the dream that would be our life as a family. I can clearly remember arriving in Mexico City. My mother was the only woman wearing trousers. I remember the stares, the disapproval. I recall with awe the huge story murals telling tales of age-old prophecies, the magic in the air.

Our family settled in Amecameca, an old Aztec village about an hour south of Mexico City. Amecameca is a little mountain pueblo nestled between the two volcanoes Popocatepetl and Iztaccihuatl. I could not have known then where my path would lead me, that years later I would become intimate with the power of the volcano in sacred marriage.

My parents and two of my older brothers took on the task of schooling Benjamin, Joseph, and me: seven, eleven, and nine years of age, respectively. We studied algebra, literature, and history. To this day I can recite the thirteen Incan kings I memorized during lessons in that Aztec village. I later had the list drummed into me with even greater incentive than intellectual interest. Several years afterward, in Kenya, my brother Michael would ask me to name the Incan leaders each morning upon arising. If I failed, I would forfeit a ride in the car and have to walk three miles to school. How was I to know that these thirteen Incas and their sacred traditions would later become a part of my life, a part of my very being?

I learned to speak Spanish, a child's conversational Spanish. My brothers and I played and were happy. Our landlady, a widow, was a proud woman, with a daughter of marriageable age who was a great beauty. Seeing that I had six brothers but no sisters, she and her daughter took me in and shared their daily creative tasks with me. They taught me to cook— fresh masa, tortillas, molé, walnut paste. I remember going with them to gather honey from their hives. They would ring a bell, and on cue the bees would magically leave the hive. I took it all in, and, as with all children, the magic became the norm, commonplace.

I quickly realized that magic in Mexico is attributed to the great mother, the feminine deity. Most of the residents of Amecameca were devout Catholics. There were shrines to the Virgin everywhere; in my eyes all those around me were worshiping the mother, the goddess. I had not been schooled in religion and our family did not worship in the traditional sense. But I absorbed it all, frequently walking down to the plaza to bask in the light inside the huge cathedral. Since those days I have often found solace in empty churches and cathedrals the world over, basking in the cool air, resting, feeling at home and at peace, from Mombasa to New York City, entering and sitting awhile as the mood took me.

The day came when my parents announced that it was time to decide where we would make our home more permanently. In the family decision of where to live next, democracy ruled. My mother and father had selected a list of possible locations for us to live—Mexico, Red China, Cuba (still forbidden by the U.S. government), Bangalore in India, and Kenya. Each family member had a vote. Benny, Joseph, and I each had one vote; the adult siblings—Stefan, Michael, Peter, and Peter's wife Joanie—had three, and my parents had five. By vote we packed up our Land Rover and headed for the coast to catch a freighter to Africa. And so it was that Benjamin, Joseph, and I were playing in the harbor in Mombasa, watching the freighter unload.

Listening to the Inner Voice

Driving northwest, we settled in an area just outside of Nairobi where there were no televisions, no toys. There was instead an abundance of the joys of life—conversation, creative play, the animal kingdom, plants, stones. As a family, we found happiness, even ecstasy. The sparkle returned to mother's eyes. All things beat with a different rhythm.

We were no longer separate from nature. On the contrary, we were reminded each and every day that we were nature, part and parcel. The bush was my classroom. Wherever we went in those early years, walking or driving, game abounded—huge herds of wildebeest, hartebeest, zebras, gazelles, buffalo, elephants, giraffes, and always the stalking lion, hyena, and vulture. The open savannah with miles of grassy plains, dusted with ancient baobab. The sun's rays beating, beating, beating, as we searched, watching for any change or movement, until in the distance we saw rising red dirt. The mass of red dust grew, expanded, closed in. Then the noise—at first barely audible, it rose to a rumbling crescendo. Then the very planet was shaking under our feet. A river of living beings was on the move, their trampling feet bringing death and birth. A newborn wildebeest, still wet from the womb, dropped without dignity into the rushing herd, standing shakily, mother long gone, moving into the sea of beasts.

Birth and death were our constant companions. Children much younger than I carried their siblings on their backs, wrapped in brightly colored *khanga* cloths. Mothers of all kinds nursed their young. Driving through the savannah, we saw giraffes birthing on the plains, the tender ten-foot-tall babies taking their first unsteady steps immediately after falling from above. At that time in Africa it was said that the crocodile was responsible for more animal-related deaths than any other, save the mosquito (I understand the hippo now holds that dubious award). During my early years in Kenya, the father of one of my friends was eaten by a crocodile. Pet dogs were taken in the dead of night by leopards. Cobras reared their heads from the grassy fields of play. There were beggars on the streets with deformed and missing limbs. Suffering, deformity, ecstasy, perfection in all things. In a literal and concrete way I experienced the finite nature of our lives and the cycle of eternity. This experiential knowing of our limited time in this life fostered living fully in the moment in a compelling way.

The endless cycle, and we were part of it! I fell in love with the land, with the people, with the energy—and with Dave Behrens. He was seventeen, a gentle giant, deeply connected with nature. He knew the name of any bird that flew, and more. We roamed about the countryside playing; observing the animals, plants, and birds; enjoying the wonders that abounded. We connected. I became pregnant.

"Pull out the champagne, Peter, I'm going to be a grandmother," my mother shouted to my brother over the telephone line from Nairobi to Paris. I had finally told her about my pregnancy. Openly joyous and supportive about the impending birth of their first grandchild, my parents privately agonized about the best course of action, about what was "right" for me, for Dave, for the child.

Dave's parents were horrified. I was ruining not only my life, but the life of their son—and their reputation. My teachers and headmaster decided that I was a poor example to the other students and that I could not return to school. My aunt advised abortion. She would take care of me in California and I could return to school. Conventional wisdom had it that my future aspirations and dreams would be limited by this "mistake," and severely so. I was told to be sensible, to see reason, to think of my future, of my family, of my child, and future children. Abort—that was the conventional wisdom.

I did see an abortionist, exploring that option, as well as the option of adoption. Carefully and diligently, Dave and I discussed and researched all of our alternatives. Only my parents were open to my own thoughts. Supportive of me in whatever decision I made, they prepared for any eventuality. Dave and I agonized for six weeks, then came to our decision—we would have the baby. A few weeks after my sixteenth birthday, my belly swollen with child, Dave and I were married by a justice of the peace. We signed the papers. There was no champagne.

Oblivious to the hardships ahead, I loved being pregnant. I even loved the act of childbirth, though my labor was long and arduous. The nurses, Irish sisters at the Matermiserichordiae Hospital, buzzed around me. "Oh, but you're just a child yourself!" they repeated over and over in their strong Irish brogue. *What could they possibly know about it, they've never given birth,* I remember thinking, between pains.

On October 20th, 1970, Kenyatta Day, Alice C'mell Behrens was born. Her middle name was taken from the name of the cat lady in a Cordwainer Smith science fiction novel. Innocent and full of hope, I had taken no notice of all the well-meant advice, or of reason. Had I been reasonable, I would have aborted and stayed in school. I had already come to question what is right and what is reasonable. I was already familiar with the duality of all of life's gifts—divine order and divine chaos.

Throughout my life, birth and death had surrounded me, educating me in the laws of nature. To which laws are we bound? Are the difficult experiences of our lives barriers or gifts? Obstacles or tests? Givers of tools that will reveal their usefulness later in life? At puberty I became a mother. Suddenly I was dismissed from high school, from social circles, from the dreams of a child. What might have been a huge obstacle was a magnificent learning experience from which I developed methods that I use and teach to this day. I took on responsibility with joy and alacrity. I learned that I could and would rise to this and any occasion.

Most of all, I learned to listen to my inner voice. Call it my conscience, my guides, my angels . . . call it what you will. I learned very young that I could count on this invisible guidance and support, even when it differed widely from conventional wisdom and from external guidance. I learned that barriers are not bad, that good comes of the process of confronting barriers, that we receive benefit from all of life's experiences.

My inner voice told me through it all that I would ultimately be fine. My inner self told me that we would all be taken care of and our needs would be met, that my aspirations not only would come to fruition, but would benefit from having and keeping this baby. At first—not secure with the advice of my inner voice—I explored the options so forcefully advised by those around me. When I finally accepted this inner voice, it stopped being advice and became a knowing. I knew not only what I must do, but what I desired—to have my baby.

I am now a mother of four, a grandmother of three. My beautiful baby girl, Alice, has been my partner through so very many life experiences, and she is now twice a mother herself. I am truly blessed, and I have a responsibility. A responsibility to share my blessings, to share the knowledge of the ways of being that allow us all to be whatever it is we choose. A responsibility to help others see that we choose our dreams, and through our dreams we create our world.

Looking Better or Seeing Better?

Beauty. Sensuality. Sexuality. Charisma. I have long questioned these notions. What are these things? Are they culturally defined? Dependent on the fashion of the time? Are they culturally, racially, or gender specific? Are there universal definitions?

During my formative years I was surrounded by the beauty of Africa—natural vistas, the savannah, the Indian Ocean, equatorial lakes, wilderness, animals, trees. And human beauty—raw, wild, sensual, sexual, exotic. Cultural diversity was a part of the daily life of my family. It seemed that there was a constant stream of guests at our home—friends, travelers we met on the streets with nowhere else to go, all kinds of people—coming and going. Somalis drinking spiced chai and chewing *qat,* Americans resting in their journeys and smoking everything, Watutsi, Zulus, Kambas, Indians, Pakistanis

. . . none were turned away. Here I learned the sacred nature of generosity and hospitality. I learned to honor the diversity of humanity. I learned that there are limitless ways of living, each "right" in its own context.

Kenya was a nation of mixed heritage, including Bantus, Nilots, Caucasians, and Asians. The tribespeople were unabashedly naked, glowing with health and vitality. The American and European expatriates of the "happy valley" days were wild in their own unique way, splashy and vibrant. The Asians were demurely sensual, flowing in multicolored silk. People adorned with tattoos, scarification, ocher, piercings, stretched and elongated earlobes, lips, and necks—testimony to rites of passage, pride, and passion.

Surrounded by these images and experiences, I formed my personal notion of beauty, while those around me formed theirs in a myriad of variations. There was no single way in which to aspire to beauty. The white women struggled to lose weight and be thin, while being attentive to their makeup, hair, jewelry, and clothes. The Bantus struggled to gain weight, heaviness being a sign of prosperity and a highly sought after, attractive characteristic in a woman. The Masai adorned their necks with circle after circle of colorful beads, the stiff beaded necklaces bouncing up and down on their bared breasts with each step. The Muslims covered as much skin as possible when out in public, all black and shrouded in the hot African sun. The Indians were wrapped in layer after layer of rich colored silk, midriffs bared, bejeweled and pierced with precious stones in their ears and noses, painted with kohl and mendhi.

As a young girl I watched as all of the women around me aspired to their own culture's definitions of beauty. I watched and questioned. What of the skinny Baganda woman who can't seem to gain weight or hasn't enough food to eat? What of the chubby European who inherited large hips and thighs, a propensity for a larger layer of fat? What of the ones whose fashion sense doesn't match that of their culture? Are they not beautiful? Are they doomed to feel that in their communities they are ugly?

The outer manifestations of striving for beauty and the rites of passage to man- and womanhood varied widely, yet the inner qualities of strength, magnetism, charisma, beauty, and sensuality were omnipresent. Notions of inner beauty crossed racial and cultural lines, regardless of the methods of external attainment. Some had all the external trappings of beauty—absolutely perfect external features—yet were not in the least beautiful, attractive, or charismatic. Others had none of the fashionable external features of beauty, yet when they walked into a room, it lit up with a brightness of pure charisma, of sensuality. Every person in the room was attracted to them, like moths to a flame, their beauty sending out waves of energy, infecting those around them with a lightness of being, smiles appearing on all faces as they came near.

What exactly is beauty?

From the perspective of a plastic surgeon, beauty is in the three-dimensional lines, the balance, the proportions. Artistic masters have written of the golden proportions for eons—the mathematical proportions that are pleasing to the eye—the balance seen throughout nature, in the curve of the nautilus shell, the spiral of the sunflower. We can take measurements as plastic surgeons: the ratio of the length of the nose to the depth; the angles; the proportion of the face from the hairline to the eyes, the eyes to the base of the nose, the nose to the chin; the projection of the chin; the distance of the helix of the ears to the scalp; the distance of the sternal notch to the nipples . . . so many measurements. Using plastic surgery, we, as surgeons, can adjust these measurements and these proportions. Does this create beauty?

What about those in our culture whom we consider beautiful? The icons? The supermodels? Do they always have these golden proportions? The answer is "No, not always." What else makes up beauty if it is not just the three-dimensional physicality, the measurements, the proportions? Think about someone you know whom you consider beautiful. What is it that makes that person beautiful?

Look at the magazines of ten and twenty years ago. Hasn't our culture's concept of even physical beauty changed? Where are the voluptuous full-figured curves of the pin-up models? Why were there only Caucasians in the older magazines? Where did the variety and the exotic looks—the full lips and high cheekbones—of today's models come from? Is this a change in our definition of human beauty or a change in perception, in the way we see?

Is beauty truly in the eye of the beholder? Can we call whatever we see beautiful, depending on our perspective? Can we enhance our looks by changing our vision? What do we all strive for? Why? I found myself asking these questions as I approached puberty in this sea of life and multiculture. It was right at puberty that I ceased being a maiden and became a mother. Pregnant at age fifteen—a short time as maiden, indeed. Later, as a plastic surgeon, a deliverer of the dream called beauty, I discovered that every woman wants to be a maiden—forever. We abhor the trappings of motherhood: the childbearing hips, the sagging breasts. As we pass through menopause, our grasping at eternal maidenhood becomes even more desperate. Where are the crones, the wise women, of our time?

Through the years I have watched how we treat the elderly in the United States, my home for a quarter of a century now, and I wonder why anyone would ever want to become a crone. The wise women (and men) are viewed as though they have long passed their time of usefulness; they are treated as dispensable, even burdensome, members of society. No wonder people come to me in droves for facelifts, eyelid surgery, laser skin resurfacing, breast augmentations and lifts, tummy tucks, liposuction. No wonder—their very place in their communities, their very ability to be perceived as a plausible and desired member of society, is at stake.

Maidens forever? Wait! Let's reassess this notion. If old women and men are not taken seriously in our culture, are maidens and warriors? What is the consequence of this tremendous block in the flow of our communal energy as we age? What are we creating for ourselves by this vision of perpetual youth? What is the essence of our dreams for ourselves, and for our children's children? What is our perception of beauty? Is beauty itself a dream, or is it a method that we hope to use to achieve another dream? If it is the latter, what is the underlying essence of the dream that is fueling our wish for beauty? Is it sex? Power? Recognition? Love? Do we strive to look better, or to see better?

Many times, while pondering these questions, I find myself journeying through the land of memory, transported to another time and place, a shamanic expedition with Dream Change Coalition, a pivotal time in my life, a deep healing in the upper Amazon region of Ecuador. I was in the courtyard outside the lodge of a great Shuar shaman, Tuntuam, dancing rhythmically under the influence of the great teacher ayahuasca. The spirit of the vine opens one's head—takes the top off—so that one can commune with the spirits. That night I was communing with the moon and the stars, the forest and the earth, and dancing, dancing, dancing.

As the night progressed, the moon came to me and said she had a gift. I thanked her and awaited the explanation with a feeling of profound gratitude. After some time she said, "I give you the gift of new eyes." I knew immediately what she was referring to—my view of the world, of life, my perspective.

The vision shifted at that point. I saw a community of people, each one glowing with an aura of vitality and purpose—children, parents, and grandparents laughing and talking as they worked. I saw Maria Juana, the shaman from the Andes. Her eyes shone through the map made by the wrinkles in her face with a beauty and passion that surpassed that of any *Vogue* model. I saw doña Amalia, the Shuar shaman and plant medicine woman, singing as she harvested healing plants, imbued with the beauty of all the earth, the beauty of the mother, the beauty of the crone. I saw my daughters playing with their daughters, dancing in the sunlight, full of their individual charismatic energy and beauty, dancing like no one was watching. I saw them reaching out to one another, and to their brothers and fathers, full of love and connection, happy and vital. I saw the essence of the dream of being human.

New eyes. Expanded perception.

"Life is the embodiment of our dreams," said the moon. "Perception defines it moment by moment."

4

Trees across the River of Life

ARE THE TREES THAT FALL across the rivers of our lives obstacles or bridges? Do they block our way or redirect flow? What leads us to lose control of our lives, of our dreams? What makes one obstacle a learning experience that aids us in building stronger tools for life, while other obstacles cause depression—a shutdown of all resources and a resignation of control? I have heard depression called the "cancer of the twenty-first century." Is depression a failure of connection with our own inner voices? Is it disconnection not only with ourselves, but with spirit, with the world—a blockage of all messages? Is it truly the loss of our dreams—dreams for ourselves, for our future, for our community, for our life? Or does depression have a purpose? Is it a message itself? These questions burned at the core of my life not long after Alice's birth, as despair slowly pervaded my family.

My mother would often tell me that "despair is the greatest sin. We have been given the gift of life, and to wallow in despair seems ungrateful to the extreme." (This is one of the tenets of Judaism, the religious tradition of my father's family.) Yet, just as despair derailed me, it also seeped into my mother's life. Although she surmounted many serious obstacles early in her life, actualizing many of her deep and true dreams, by the time of my remembering my mother would go to work and go to bed. Her spirit was already breaking under the strain of her work as a doctor. She had lost touch with her dreams.

My mother had always loved dancing and music—Benny Goodman and Bessie Smith. Passion for life and love coursed her veins, and she pushed the limits of existence wherever she found herself, trying everything at least once. An avid reader, she would quote Blake, Thomas, Rimbaud, Lorca, all in their original tongues.

Her sister Eve was head welder in the San Francisco dockworkers' union during World War II. She was a great beauty who later became the top salesperson for New York Life. This afforded her and her sons a "life on the hill," complete with a spectacular home in Sausalito overlooking the Golden Gate Bridge, and three Jaguars—a red one, a white one, and a blue one. I adored my Aunt Eve, my namesake, affectionately known as Sissy. She has been a guide and inspiration to me in life, and that relationship has only deepened since her death. Practical, pragmatic, and successful, she was also flashy, stylish, creative, zestful, fun-loving, caring, and dedicated to her family. She often comes to me as a spirit guide at difficult times.

My mother's other sister, Aunt Barbara, did not like to mingle with those "on the hill." Kicked out of college for wearing a hip flask and smoking a cigar, she continued her bohemian lifestyle to her death. Always a strong proponent for human rights, she never backed down in the face of opposition. From her I learned to stand up for human rights and dignity at all costs, to speak my truth and be true to my words, even in the face of hardship and controversy. She also taught me to keep in mind the perspective of interconnectedness, of how everyone is affected by any action or thought, to always remember community, honor, and decency even if it means that the "outer package" of life is compromised by that perspective. She gave me the tool of cutting through to the essence, of never giving up, and of being rather than seeming.

These three women pushed the limits, living fervently on the edge. Yet I understand now that at some point there was a major change in my mother. Many years later my brother Peter—fifteen years my senior— was telling stories of her dancing, passionate, full of life. At that moment I had a sad realization—"We had a different mother!" I cried. Over the years something had been crushed; depression had set in. Yet she worked effectively through it all, continuing as a vital contributor to her profession.

Recently my father's cousin Ted told me a story of being treated by my mother many years ago. He had developed severe, debilitating pain in his jaw. Ted saw dentist after puzzled dentist, and one finally extracted a tooth. "He examined it, smelled it, and said, 'Ted, this is a perfectly healthy tooth. There's nothing wrong with it.'" Then Ted went to a series of internists. He was finally referred to a neurologist and diagnosed with neuralgia. Surgery was scheduled on the affected nerve, though he was told of the risk of a droopy eye postoperatively. "By that time," he said, " I wouldn't have cared if I went blind in the eye! The pain was excruciating and unending!" When he visited our home the day before his surgery, my mother noticed his discomfort. "What's the matter, Teddy?" she asked. He told her of his problem, and she said "I can fix that if you'll give me ten days. I'll have to give you shots every day, though." He told me that at that point he just wanted it stopped as soon as possible, but his wife persuaded him to try the shots, and thereby avoid the risk of an eye disfigurement. "Every day I went to your house, or to her office. Every day she'd give me two shots in the butt, both at the same time. Your mom wasn't much for messing around. Get it done, and get it done right! By the tenth day the pain wasn't gone, but it was much better. A week after the series of shots, the pain was completely gone. I was so happy. She told me that it would return, and that when it did, to remember the shots. She was right, and from time to time over the years I would return to her for treatment."

Ted told me that when he was transferred to another state and moved, he carefully wrote down the combination of medications that my mother used. He continued, "Sure enough, one day I had another episode. I took the names of the shots to an internist that I knew and trusted. He said 'Teddy, this won't do anything for you.' I pleaded with him and insisted on getting the shots, and it worked so well that he uses that regimen to this day on his own patients. He was astounded. Your mother was something else!"

Treatment by chemical manipulation is fast and effective. It works. For my mother, an empiricist always, chemical manipulation was just one more effective method of controlling disease, of fixing things. She was a child of modern medicine, of the era of quantum leaps in the field of pharmacology. In her time the pharmacopoeia expanded exponentially, as did our philosophy of treating disease—from the advent of penicillin to the linking of mental disease with chemical imbalance.

Chemicals had become a way of life and our culture's preferred method for treatment. Chemical alteration, chemical cures, chemical fixes—hers was the pill-popping generation. If you get sick, take a pill. If you are a doctor and you diagnose an illness, write a prescription and send the patient home to take it. If there is a disease without a known cure, search in the laboratory for a chemical. She practiced medicine in the age that was enthralled with this new form of healing, which expanded in scope daily. Some even wondered if it was the final answer to all of our ills. By the time I hit adolescence, I was aware that my mother was treating herself for fatigue. By then she was a board-certified pathologist—the sole pathologist for the Rift Valley Province of over a million people—and her workload was staggering. It was the sixties, the time of "pep pills." Women all over the industrialized world were trying to enhance their energy and vitality with amphetamines, and my mother was no exception.

By the time I was thirteen, I was also frequenting altered states, with the help of marijuana, hashish, uppers, and downers. Like many of that age, I turned to drugs, sex, and rock and roll in my pursuit of happiness. As expatriate children in Kenya, we had too much free time, too little opportunity for purposeful work, too much freedom to experiment. Our drug-induced visions and trips drenched us in colors, feelings, emotions, and new experiences. We learned about new eyes, about seeing the same world with different eyes, about the possibility of having different perceptions of the same reality. That sent us on a search for the "best eyes," for ecstasy. Our drug use spiraled as we searched—opium, heroin, quaaludes, dexamphetamine, methamphetamine, LSD, cocaine, combinations, designer drugs. We denounced those that came before us and their old dreams as we sought a new dream for humanity with our chemically altered perceptions. But happiness was elusive. We were dreaming, dreamshaping, but we were crippled in our ability to effectively change our dream. What were we missing? While we were so busy living in an altered state, was life passing us by? We were confused about our intent and our destination. In our drive to escape, we didn't know where we were headed. As we walked through life getting high, many of us walked into death. It was a common occurrence to hear of friends overdosing.

My unplanned pregnancy brought me rapidly to my senses. It was a gift, a message. I stopped ingesting compulsively, and I found a beauty surrounding me that I had been missing in my pursuit, a life that I was not living. Suddenly devoid of chemically induced visions, I could see as if for the first time the splendors around me—the plants, the animals, the clouds, the Great Rift Valley, the tribespeople, the Indian Ocean, the white sands, the savannah. All my senses came alive again to the aromas, the textures, the music, the tastes. I was pregnant with time on my hands, and I learned the art of food-shaping, the creativity of combined tastes and textures. The world that we had chemically tried to escape was indeed a delight!

Spiraling into Darkness

But our family was headed for another unseen challenge; we were to face more trees across the river of our lives. The three youngest children of the family—my brothers Benny and Joe and I—had gone to British schools in Africa. The British environment had been strange to us, yet we adjusted as children do, absorbing Latin, English history, Swahili, geometry, and drama. We played hockey, rounders, cricket, and tennis. Benny was two years younger than I was, and Joseph was two years older. Joe was an extrovert— he played all out, had friends of his own, things to do, places to go. Benny and I shared a world of our own. He was my closest friend. I remember a time when we created a language, both spoken and written, that only the two of us could understand. Gentle and sensitive, he was blessed with great creative genius. We captured images with our cameras and developed them in our own darkroom, learning the power of creation together. We played endless games with music and fantasy, partners in a strange new world. I remember those days with gentle fondness, through fading memories, veiled but distinctly pleasant. To a child, all experience is at one and the same time miraculous and normal. We develop our concept of normalcy and reality through our childhood experiences.

It was again my oldest brother, Peter, who, many years later, opened my eyes to seeing Benny's childhood from a different perspective. He spoke of being aware of Benny's difficulties at school, at play, and in social situations. When he told me that he knew then that there was something awry, I was shocked by his revelation! To me, Benny and I were the absolute index of normality until well after puberty, when Benny began to falter in his attempts to find a way of functioning in society.

It was right around the time that I became pregnant with Alice that his condition became untenable. I will forever wonder whether there was a connection between these two major life events. Did Alice come to help me with the loss of Benny? Did I turn to Dave to attempt to avoid the unavoidable that was developing before my eyes in his suffering and fall from sanity?

To me, there was no clue, no warning. Yes, he was eccentric perhaps, but it was the sixties, and everyone was a little strange. Then he increasingly began to have trouble with school, with the law, with society. My sweet brother Benjamin crossed over. The diagnosis was schizophrenia. I learned of the fragility of our minds—intangible, uncontrollable. I watched helplessly as he fell, spiraling deeper and deeper into madness, despair, and rage.

The whole family joined in my mother's desperate efforts to "cure" him, to abate his symptoms in any and every way available. We grappled with the disease for many years, eventually leaving Kenya and our dreams there to try to find help for him in the medical community in the United States. My parents—who had forsaken their homeland and the American dream for a chance at a broader dream, for the passion of life abroad—returned in desperation, seeking any help they could find. Determined, they fought bravely and incessantly for his health, a fierce and determined battle. Medication, wheat-free diet, institutions, therapy, electric shock treatments— you name it, we tried it. My mother was fighting the battle of her life . . .

and losing. In the end, she surrendered. She gave in; we gave up. We couldn't fix this one. Not with all that medicine had to offer. Not even by searching for a cure outside of conventional medicine. Not by listening to our hunches, our inner voices. Not with any amount of strength and determination. Not even by letting go.

Our dream for him was not his dream, it seemed. His dream was un-fathomable to us. The life he was living was certainly not easy for him. He was in and out of institutions. He was full of rage and unhappy by anyone's definition. What was his dream? What was his message? Our message? And what about me? Did my experience with him—my understanding, tolerance, and love for him—prepare me for listening to many differing perspectives and realities later in life?

Vision or Madness?

Sometimes I wonder if it would have been easier for Benny if he had been a part of a different, more tolerant community. Would his "disease" have been accepted as I accepted him in my childlike innocence? Would his rantings and ravings have been listened to? If he had been listened to and heard, would he still have experienced the profound anger that filled his days? After surrendering the battle, my parents moved with Benny to Hawaii. Here they found a more tolerant culture and society. My parents' neighbors on Oahu, where they made their home in the early 1970s, were a Hawaiian couple who fought ferociously and daily. The police were called to stop them more nights than not. Yet one day, when my parents came home, they found the husband sitting at the table reading gently to Benny from the Bible. Although Benny was never functional or what society would call "normal" again, his insanity was tolerated more freely and gently in Hawaii than on the mainland. Even in the face of their defeat at finding a cure, my parents continued to do the best they could for him. They gave him a home and their unfaltering love. And still he denounced everything about them and his home, forever unhappy with wherever he was at the moment, his angry outbursts landing him in and out of institutions even in the more tolerant atmosphere of the Hawaiian Islands.

If he had been a part of a tribal culture such as that of the Shuar, would Benny have been able to live out a life, one of fantasy perhaps, yet a life within the community? Or could he even have been fully functioning, with his own niche and purpose in society, even looked to for his visions and voices? I don't fully know the answer to these questions, but some light was thrown on them when John Perkins told me about an experience he'd had. One day, he was going down the Amazon River in a canoe with a shaman who was his teacher. They passed a disheveled man on the banks of the river who was obviously psychotic—ranting and raving wildly. "Is that a shaman?" asked John.

"Oh no." said the shaman. "That man is crazy."

We may perhaps be indulging in a sentimental or romantic notion when we think that insanity would be a benefit in performing shamanic work. Certainly important "psychotic" episodes are described and expected in deepening spiritual connection, but there may be a difference between these spiritual experiences and madness. I have struggled to understand the distinction between the times when it is necessary to take control and the times when we benefit from letting go. In the process of creating change and manifesting our dreams, how can we find the balance? What is the difference between letting go, flowing with grace, and losing control, going crazy? I have sometimes faced the fearful question—could I go crazy, too? Could I let go without fear of falling into deep dysfunctional madness like my brother?

At the University of Maryland, where I later obtained my M.D., there was a renowned researcher in the field of schizophrenia, Dr. Carpenter. I remember his distinctions well. He described the symptoms of schizophrenia as positive and negative. The positive symptoms were those for which there was available pharmacological treatment, such as auditory and visual hallucinations. However, there was no available treatment for the negative symptoms, such as the lack of enthusiasm, ambition, social interaction, and connection. Listening to this and remembering the change in Benny, I felt that the negative symptoms can be seen in a schizophrenic's eyes—the lack of a soul, the lack of life force, the lack of personal dreams.

Is this where the difference lies? Is it that the positive symptoms—when expressed with passion and ambition, with dreams—signify more of a spiritual event, whereas these same symptoms—when combined with the negative over many years—signify schizophrenia? Could it be a choice, could it be the dream of the one who goes crazy? Or is it an extreme loss of balance between the divine life force and the persona that is the ghost of our limited existence in this life? And if it is an imbalance of soul and spirit, what is gone, the spirit or the soul?

For many years I visited Benny in various institutions, and after each visit we would both be left traumatized. One time he asked, "If one of us kids had to go crazy, why did it have to be me?"

"I don't know, Benny. I don't know."

After a time I realized that it was painful for him to see me, and painful for me, too. I was haunted by the unknown: Why did I go? What was the responsible thing to do? How could I help him? Was it my responsibility to help him, and what if I couldn't? Or worse, what if I was making it harder for him? Benny now lives in a lockup institution in the Bay Area in California, overseen by my brother Joseph, who serves as his unfaltering conservator. Over the years his extreme volatility and anger have mellowed some, but his dysfunction in society continues.

Years later, sitting with the great high holy man, prophet, and healer Vusamazulu Credo Mutwa in South Africa, we talked about insanity. "A healer must always look for the door that every crazy person is holding open for them," he explained. "When you find the door, you can enter his or her world and begin the healing process, but never by trying to force the crazy person through the door back into our world.

"One day I was in Zimbabwe and I was taken to a home to heal the daughter of the chief. I was told that she was crazy, and none of the healers or doctors had been able to do anything for her.

"I walked in and found a girl in chains. 'Unchain her!' I demanded of them. Reluctantly they unchained her, saying that she was violent and had injured many people in times past.

"Imagine my surprise when I heard this village girl begin to speak English with a Southern drawl! I had been to the United States and spoke English well. I know the customs of the South, but her family and villagers thought that she was speaking jibberish. 'Nigger,' she called to me. 'Come here, boy. Don't look at me like that.'

"Seeing the door, I answered as a slave would 'Yes, ma'am,' and approached her. We conversed in this way for weeks. She told me that her beau had gone to war and had promised to return, but had left her in this horrible place. Finally one day a letter came. She asked me to read it to her. I told her it was a letter announcing that her beau had died a hero's death and was being honored. At that moment she snapped back and couldn't understand a word I was saying. Speaking again in her native tongue, she asked me who I was and what I was doing visiting her father's house. From that day on she was completely sane, and the chief was very happy with me, I can tell you that."

Find the door. I wonder if I could have found a door for Benny in the years when we were younger. I had certainly searched for one long and hard. It was Benny's illness that spurred my first desperate questioning of the nature of healing and of health. Those painful doubts are echoed by questions that I have often struggled with as a doctor. Why do some of us get certain challenges, certain limitations, while others don't? Can we "fix" everything if we try hard enough? Is that the nature of healing? Do all diseases and limitations need curing to find health? Is health the same for everyone, or as individual as our lives, as our bodies, as our souls? Who are we helping, anyway? What is our deep motivation? Is it more for the patient or for our own ego? Do we sometimes worsen the situation, create more disease, by trying so hard to fix things to match our definition of the way it should be?

These spoken and unspoken questions rocked my world as my brother Benny retreated from us into raging insanity and my mother sank into quiet desperation. This was something she couldn't fix, that none of us could fix, no matter how bravely or powerfully we fought. Despair settled in for a very long time.

What was the battle? What is the battle? Who are we fighting? What is the war? The shadows of these questions deepened as I lost touch with my own dreams, as I lost my own soul, following Benny into deep despair, full of the negative symptoms that were his domain, but without the fire of the positive symptoms. I became a shell, one of the walking dead, not schizophrenic and not fully alive. Although my struggle to listen to my inner voice through Alice's birth had taught me that what appears to be an obstacle can become an opportunity, that early lesson faded as I lost a clear vision of my personal dream.

A Dream Derailed

As a child I dreamed of being an animal behaviorist. I was friends with many people in the field, such as David Hopcraft, and exposed frequently to many others, such as Jane Goodall and Iain and Oria Douglas-Hamilton. I had no doubts that this was what I would do after completing my schooling. I pictured my future quite clearly, camera and notebook handy, sitting for hours in the bush observing the behavior of animals, learning their ways of communing with each other, their hearts, their souls, the workings of the natural world. This was my dream, and when I was dismissed from school, it seemed to me that the dream was simply put on hold. And yet, the business of being a mother, of being responsible for the daily nourishment and well-being of first Alice and then a second child, Michael Dylan, born three years later, began to shift my view of my ability to realize any dream of my own. I had become a mother, happily and joyfully, and I discovered firsthand what that identity takes from one's persona, from one's personal dreams. No longer a single entity, a self alone with selfish desires, I abdicated to my children's well-being. I thought that this was a minor delay in the dream that was Eve, and it may have been. Our dreams for our lives are naturally clothed in different language and concepts as we grow and change, but there is usually a core that is expressed differently in different time frames.

The marriage born from young love began to falter, and Dave and I grew apart in every way possible. Wanting to continue my schooling so that I could support my children, I returned to the United States and enrolled in science classes after taking the GED high school equivalency test. My advisors at school saw my aptitude and recommended premed. With just a little hesitation I forsook the dreams of my early years and, following in my mother's footsteps, set out to complete my studies for becoming a doctor, so that I could begin earning for my family as rapidly as possible. Yet over time I was to realize that dreams given up too easily have a way of haunting us incessantly in the depths of our subconscious. When one of our dreams is killed and dies without proper grief and respect, something important in us also dies. I forgot my early hard-earned lessons and the strength of life passion I had gained from my inner voice. I buried that voice in order to be "sensible," to live my life in a way that I was told would be best for my children, for I was caring for them on my own. My concern for them led me to doubt the path that I had dreamed of following and to search for another.

While I was on this new path, this search for a "better" life for my children, the shell that I had become—the me without a personal dream, without passion—met and fell in love with another man. My second husband, McDonnell Bruce, seemed to have it all—he was bright, articulate, gregarious, fun-loving, handsome. Born with a silver spoon in his mouth, he had a background that was blue-blood social registry. He came from a close-knit and wonderful adoring family. His father, Dan Bruce, started the first photographic safari company in Kenya. His mother is Betty Leslie Melville, a successful author and celebrity known as "the giraffe lady." Inseparable at the beginning, we loved each other deeply, and his family became mine in every way. He approved wholeheartedly of my new dream and of the life that I was busy building. I felt that I was happy, but my soul—the persona that I had killed in forsaking my passion—was not embodied in that life, and the happiness was but a reflection of my family's wishes.

Working toward the dream of financial and social success, we struggled through the long years of university, and then my medical school and residency. McDonnell studied film and became an editor, then joined his family in the safari business, and finally realized his own passion as a chef.

All the while, I plodded up the ladder of "success." Along the rungs of this ladder there were many signs. In my year as chief resident in general surgery I was pregnant with my third child, our daughter Coale. In my year as chief resident in plastic surgery, I was pregnant with my fourth child, our son Jock. The pattern was striking. Were these beautiful children of mine my true dreams? Were they messages from my inner voice imploring me to listen? Was I unconsciously trying to sabotage the "dream" life I thought I was creating for my children and for McDonnell, that of a successful doctor, at the cost of my own dreams, and of my soul?

At this point in my life I was closed to all of these possibilities. I entered deep despair. I had lost sight of my personal dream and became deaf to my inner voice. Without this internal guidance, without a clear dream, I found myself subjugating my wishes to what I perceived to be those of my family, and of our culture at large. Outwardly McDonnell and I were the perfect couple, with success, love, family, recognition, and material goods. Inwardly the subjugation of our personal dreams had rendered both of us deaf to our inner voices—and to our souls.

In the end, our marriage failed. After my first divorce, I had sworn to myself that I would never go through that pain again, but this time I learned that we can walk through the pain into a world of vast possibility. My own life taught me that however impossible or painful the situation, no matter how high the wall, our dreams can come true, if we choose to believe in them. We ourselves are the only limit to the power of our dreams and our creative potential. We need only take the steering wheel of our dreams and aspirations in our hands with conscious intent. Yes, there will be walls, pain, obstacles, but my experiences at the time of my second divorce clearly taught me that whatever the obstacle confronting us at any given time, it may truly be a gift.

A Balance of Power

In the turmoil that was my life at the end of my second marriage, I embarked on the Dream Change Coalition journey that took me to the Quechua shaman high in the Andes where I was healed. Later on the same trip I came to know the Shuar, a tribe inhabiting the area of Ecuador where the headwaters of the Amazon run down from the Andean peaks. Little is written about the tribes populating this vast area of rainforest—remote, lush, teaming with botanical and animal life. The Shuar way of life and view of the world exemplify the teaching that our obstacles may be gifts. My time with them reawakened me to my inner voice, reconnecting me with my soul.

Like the Quechua of the Andes, the Shuar people live and breathe spirituality. Spirit is part of every thought, every dream—awake and asleep—every action. The dream world is just as important as the tangible world, and nighttime dreams are discussed with family and friends at every opportunity. To the people of the Amazon, everything is sacred: every rock, every tree, every bug, every bird, every animal, every cloud, every rainbow, every moment, every word, every bite of food, every song, every dance. Every day—each moment—is a celebration. The Shuar know that we are all one. Thanks are given for all experiences, all food, all water, all life. No one takes more than they need, and something is always offered back to Mother Earth in return.

At the same time, the Shuar people have been feared for many hundreds of years, with good reason. It has been said that they are the only tribe of the Americas—North, Central, and South—who have never been conquered. Not that it hasn't been tried. The Shuar are headhunters, head-shrinkers. If you have ever seen a shrunken head in a book or a museum, it was probably taken and shrunken by a Shuar, and, in addition, it was likely to have been a Shuar head! Their oral history includes the story of an uprising against the Spaniards, who are said to have exacted taxes in gold from the Shuar for a time. The Shuar fought hard against the injustice, killing thousands of Spaniards until only two remained alive, a priest and the governor. They kept the priest alive to tell the tale, to return with the story of the Shuar victory. But they held down the governor, pried open his mouth with the bones of his wife, and poured molten gold down his throat, saying, "You asked for gold. For your greed, we give you this gold!" After that, they were never bothered much by attempts at conquest, at least in war. Conquest by cultural breakdown is another story.

During the war of Ecuador against Peru, the Shuar were used on the frontline. Fierce warriors, they consider death an honor, a shapeshift into another form, one that rises above the human form in every way. Their fearlessness makes them formidable opponents, as do their skills at hand-to-hand battle. The first time I visited Miazal, a community where traditional Shuar ways are retained, far to the east of the Cutucuu mountain range, I saw linear tattoos on the thigh of Mariano Chumpi, a Shuar warrior. "What do those lines stand for?" I asked. "Each line stands for a Peruvian that I killed," he answered. "Though I'm not sure why we had to kill each other," he admitted.

Nicknamed "Mr. December" by us gringos, this warrior is visually gorgeous! Short in stature, the Shuar are nevertheless absolutely stunning in appearance. High cheekbones, dark and handsome, compact and muscular, their physiques, both male and female, rival any model's. Yet there is more to their magnetic appeal than their physical appearance. It didn't take me long to discover what it is.

In Shuar culture, it is considered very rude to look the opposite sex directly in the eye, that is, unless you are asking someone to have sex with you. Sex in Shuar culture is enjoyed and cherished. One day a member of one of the Dream Change Coalition groups asked Mariano and his wife a question: "What do you most enjoy doing with your time?" she asked. "We enjoy everything," they quickly answered, with great sincerity. "Okay," she retorted, "but if you had to choose among activities, what do you enjoy the very most?" They looked at each other briefly, as if this was a very silly question, and replied together, "Why, making love, of course; we make love all the time."

And not just with each other. A couple of times a year the Shuar traditionally have a huge ceremony. All the men line up on one side of a lodge, the women on the other. The dancing begins. One by one a woman or man will catch the eyes of someone of the opposite sex, and off into the jungle they go for a night of lovemaking. When we explained that there is no outlet like that for extramarital or open sex in our culture, they were appalled. "You must have many sexual problems in your culture," they exclaimed with great concern. "Oh, yes," I stated truly, "we do!"

The Shuar have very strict and detailed separation of tasks between the sexes. The women are the nurturers. They work closely with Nunqui, the goddess of the earth who resides in the roots by day and comes out to dance and play among the trees by night. They sing to Nunqui while cultivating the soil or gathering food or medicinal plants. Nunqui teaches them how to care for the plants and to honor her, as goddess of the earth and all that exists. Women are the only ones permitted to prepare or even touch *chicha*, the staple diet of the Shuar. Made of manioc or yucca, chicha is prepared by chewing the root at length, then spitting this premasticated material into a container to ferment into a weak yet thick yeasty-tasting beer. This high-carbohydrate drink is the staple diet of adults and children alike, and the average adult male Shuar is said to drink several gallons of chicha a day. Each home has a chicha of slightly varying flavor, a source of great pride. It is an extreme insult to refuse to drink the chicha offered, and insulting a head-shrinker is not a sensible or healthy activity! As the woman is the only one allowed to touch or prepare the staple diet, a man could starve without a woman, or if he annoys his woman by something he does.

The men, by contrast, are not only the warriors but also the destroyers in every way. They are the hunters. They bring in the protein by hunting the birds, rodents, pigs, and monkeys of the jungle. In the times of the head-hunting wars, the average Shuar killed about six men and raised about six children to adulthood. As humans have no natural predators, this kept a good balance in the population. Since the head-hunting wars were outlawed, the jungle has suffered. The population has grown exponentially, and the jungle can no longer support the swelling ranks of the Shuar, resulting in a people who now have to resort to any way—however degrading or destructive—to obtain some cash to survive. The traditional ways are being diluted, and many say the people suffer.

I was quick to notice that although the separation of tasks between the sexes is well delineated, both are necessary. When asked which sex is considered superior among the Shuar, Mariano looked puzzled. "Superior?" he queried. "Both are essential. How can one live without the other?" Both sexes are necessary, both honored. The clear delineation of tasks removes ambiguity and fosters freedom. What stands out is that there is clear male energy in all women and female energy in all men. The balance of masculine and feminine in both the men and the women, and the clear understanding that both are necessary, both are to be honored, engenders a community with magnetic appeal, a magnetism felt both sensually and in every human way. The Shuar are a heartfelt community possessing both power and compassion. They have been my teachers for many years, and I know them as beautiful, honorable, and loving people.

These fierce male head-hunting warriors are the most gentle, caring people I know. Always there to lend a helping hand, to listen to a concern or story, to hold a baby, to laugh and roll around on the ground with the children in play, these men openly display enormous female energy.

The women who create the children and the food, who nurture the people and the earth, are as strong as any man I know. Imbued with great strength physically, mentally, and emotionally, they can handle any eventuality with grace and ease. Never faltering under any "hardship," they live life fully with unabashed power. One of the ways their feminine power is used in this community is to control the men.

I want to repeat this, because at first glance it may sound trivial: One of the ways their feminine power is used in this community is to control the men. By *control* I don't mean that women use their power to get their own way, as we often see in the endless dance of sexual power in relationships in our culture. It is not the dynamic of withholding sexual favor in order to obtain things, not the power play of "one-upmanship."

By *control* I mean the way the women fulfill their role as the nurturers, the ones who are taught by and who honor Nunqui, the earth, and all that exists, the balance of creation over destruction. In Shuar culture it is the women who are turned to for wisdom. The women are the ones who say, "We don't need a larger house; don't clear any more trees" or "We have enough to eat; don't kill more animals." It is known that if the women fall short of their responsibility to Nunqui and don't let the men know when enough destruction has occurred, Nunqui and the earth and humanity will suffer in return.

In our culture, who says when enough is enough? What happened when the focus of culture shifted from fertility and goddesses to male domination, to dominion over the earth? Where is the nurturing? Where is the control? Where is the wisdom? When is enough enough? Who suffers from the dominion and destruction?

We Are All One

On my first Dream Change Coalition trip to the Amazon, led by John Perkins, I was with fifteen other curious travelers. After our first healing experiences in the Andes, we were full of questions about shamans and their healing practices. On our bus ride down the Pastaza River canyon, John patiently answered our questions, telling us that that the best short description of a shaman is someone who not only psychonavigates or journeys to other realities, but does so in order to obtain knowledge, energy, and power to effect change in this reality. The nature of the change in this reality is as varied as healing physical illness, bringing luck in material wealth or love, and beckoning rain in times of drought.

John told us that the Shuar often say, "The world is as you dream it," and that the Shuar shamans are masters of shapeshifting.*

Shapeshifting is a shamanic term—first used by the Celts—that refers to changing one's shape, such as when the ancient Celtic shamans changed into birds or fish or oak trees, or when an Amazonian shaman turns into a jaguar or a bat. Later, I learned that we shapeshift whenever we make a physical or emotional change—when we age, gain or lose weight, become ill or get better; when we eat and the cells and molecules of our once living food become us; when we die and our cells and molecules become another.

Partly to keep my mind off the agoraphobic descent as we careened down the serpentine canyon road, I asked John to define shapeshifting for us.

"You could break shapeshifting down into three forms," he explained. "Cellular, such as when a tumor grows or shrinks; personal, such as when someone overcomes an addiction; and institutional, such as when a business

---

*For more information, please refer to *Shapeshifting* by John Perkins (Destiny Books, 1997).

adopts more sustainable practices, or like the progressive changes that occur in medicine and the healing arts.

"Shapeshifting is shifting energy. Einstein told us that everything is
energy. Bohm told us that the whole is in each part, emphasizing the holographic principle of our oneness. This truth is known by shamans the world
over, as well as by Buddhists and Hindus—we are truly one—and this is
the key to shapeshifting. The Dalai Lama says that the minds of all sentient beings are the Creator, and that is why the Buddha stated that we are
our own masters."

As we listened to John, we were filled with a new wonder—can we
change shape using the creations of our mind's eye? Can we build our world
with our dreams?

By the time we reached the Shuar, I had a vague sense that I was about
to experience another shapeshift, another quantum leap in understanding
the world, one that would expand the box of what I "know" to be true, of
what I didn't know I didn't know—an internal shapeshift.

Juan Gabriel and John spoke in hushed tones to the shaman Daniel
Wachapa as he prepared for the night of ceremony and healing. Shuar
shamans do their healing work at night, surrounded by the loud symphony of the nighttime forest. The jungle canopy hides the sky, but if you
can find a clearing, the stars are as magical and numerous as I remember
on the plains of my African childhood. Spirits are everywhere; magic
abounds. One reason that the Shuar heal at night is that they use ayahuasca
in healing ceremonies. To the Shuar, and to all the peoples of the upper
Amazon, ayahuasca is the most sacred of plants—a great teacher that
opens you up to an expanded reality and gives you new eyes forever. This
expansion continues for a lifetime, although the initial effects of the plant
last for about five hours, including hallucination and night vision, as well
as the nausea, vomiting, and diarrhea. It is not a means to escape reality;
the visions that it brings take one deeper into reality, to an understanding
of the life of the soul.

Although the Shuar and the Quechua always honor the sacred, I was
to find that they are seldom solemn. Catching up on the time since they

had last been together, John, Juan Gabriel, and Daniel laughed and joked around. They soaked strong Amazonian tobacco in water to be used as snuff. Finally the shaman carefully poured his dose of ayahuasca from the batch he had spent the day ceremoniously preparing specifically for our group, and the candles were blown out. The only light was from the perpetual fire burning near the central pole of the lodge.

One by one the anxious group members came before the shaman, announcing to him their intention for the healing and for the night, some swallowing a cup of ayahuasca, some not. Finally it was my turn. Juan Gabriel leaned in close.

"What do you want out of the healing?"

"I would like my soul back," I replied. Grasping the carefully poured cup of ayahuasca in my hands, I said a little prayer and gulped the thick, muddy, bitter fluid, chasing it with a gulp of trago (sacred sugarcane alcohol).

Later, as I studied further and witnessed and experienced many shamanic healings, I became familiar with the concept of soul retrieval. In shamanic terms, disease—even physical disease—has a spiritual basis. It begins as a spiritual imbalance, becoming physical only after much time if balance is not restored. Health can be restored only after restoring balance. This is the basis of shamanic healings. Soul loss is thought to be a common source of spiritual imbalance. Loss of portions of the soul can happen at times of trauma. The degree of trauma necessary to cause a soul loss varies widely from person to person and from time to time. The soul loss creates a hole or a space that will often be filled up with unwanted and unwelcome entities or energies. In indigenous shamanic communities, soul loss is generally recognized immediately and the soul part retrieved. In our culture, there are often years between loss and retrieval, if, indeed, the lost part is ever recovered.

That night I found myself deep in the jungle, far from my family and home, with no idea of the shamanic view of healing, asking for a soul retrieval! Looking back on it later, I realized that my soul was lost when I murdered my dream and lost the passion in life that the Shuar refer to as Arutam—the life force, the mana, the divine spark, the fire in the belly,

God. I was here to find Arutam, and my life had led me to this lodge in the middle of the Amazonian jungle with the shaman Daniel Wachapa, the perfect place to be for my purpose.

We all sat in quiet anticipation while Wachapa chanted. Intermittently the chanting was interrupted by the sound of retching and vomiting as my fellow travelers started to feel the gastrointestinal effects of the herb. I began to feel extreme nausea. Going out into the forest, I knelt to vomit, but nothing but dry heaves came for what seemed like hours. I tried to stand and started to spin. I bent over and a river of projectile vomit purged from deep within me. I watched as this stream of fluid, in my night vision, became pink. It then clearly congealed into a pile of writhing snakes. I was terrified and fascinated at the same time. I leaned forward to touch them and then—poof!—they vanished.

Now the experience shifted gears. I felt one with all around me, pure ecstasy. This is what I had only imagined heaven could be, and it was real. In the distance I heard more retching and some crying. A strong sense of empathy and compassion flowed through me, through us all, for we were no longer separate. I was the others, they were me, we were the trees, the air, the moon, the stars. I was filled with happiness, bliss, joy, sadness, all at once, simultaneously.

I was led to the shaman for my healing. I lay on the bench, and Wachapa sat on the stool in front of me. We were flying together. He started chanting and rhythmically brushing me with leaves he had carefully selected from the jungle. I saw him become a giant anaconda, then erupt into a volcano. The leaves became hummingbirds and surrounded me with a myriad of wings, beating and caressing me. Surprisingly, I found myself flying swiftly down a long tunnel. It was dark, but I could see that I was passing a succession of glowing gold-colored objects that appeared Incan in shape. This went on for weeks, at least in dreamtime, but at last I came to the end of the tunnel. Here a huge golden throne awaited my arrival. Climbing onto my throne, I rested—content, at peace in ecstatic knowing, whole. Whole in oneness, whole in spirit, whole in life force and passion. We were one—the jungle, the people, God, Arutam.

The next day, my fellow travelers came up to me one by one, each one commenting on how different I looked. "Your eyes!" they said. "Wow!"

Wow! I had shapeshifted, and my world would never be the same. I had retrieved my soul and was given the gift of the divine life force, Arutam.

I had shared the vision of the shamans: that we are all one.

5

The Path of the Shaman

WHEN I RETURNED from my first trip to Ecuador with the gift of the spark of Arutam, my perspective had shifted so much that everything in my life looked different to me. Passion returned. I knew that I had taken on a very different aura, and that people looked at me in a new way. In my first encounter with the shamans of the Amazon, I had slipped easily into a journey after saying that I wanted my soul back. That journey transformed my vision and my life. I shapeshifted in every way—emotionally, mentally, physically, and spiritually.

I resumed my practice and discovered that I was able to share new perspectives on change with my patients, helping them see that they were at a magical gateway in their lives. I was able to help them define their dreams, physical and otherwise, with more clarity and purpose. I was facilitating transformation, and I wanted to learn more. I knew that I had to return to South America, but first I needed to flex the newfound muscles that had lain dormant for so long, to begin to journey for myself and for others, and to develop deeper connections with my guides and the world around me.

Following the path that lay before me, I signed up for a workshop with John Perkins. We spent the first day focusing on introductions to each other and to our spirit guides. The second day we reconvened around the altar, which was set with representations of the elements fire, air, water, and earth and with huacas—objects that were sacred to us and with which we all had a personal relationship. John explained that journeying—the trance state that shamans have traditionally used to access other worlds or realms—could be simply defined as lucid dreaming. Although journeying is different from nighttime dreaming, like dreaming, it comes quite naturally. We settled into comfortable positions around the room and prepared to journey as the drumming began. It was time to explore our inner selves, time for each of us to confer with our own guides.

Walking between the drumbeats, I journeyed deeper and deeper, finding myself arriving at a meadow high in the mountains. The air felt cool and invigorating, smelling of fresh grass and moss. The trickling sound of a brook made harmonious music with the trill of the birds flying overhead. At this altitude, the sun's rays beat fiercely down on my skin, and I could feel the heat of the fire energy enter my spirit, imbuing me with great power as I lay on the soft grass. I became aware of icy water flowing through my fingers as they dangled over the edge of the grassy embankment into running water. I heard a low growl, and the smell of feline fur wafted into my senses. Turning abruptly, I saw my guide—a huge male lion with a scarred face and a full dark mane—my close friend, teacher, and ally. I ran over to him and buried my face in his mane. He licked me all over, like a mother cat does her kittens, cleansing me of all recent distress, releasing tightness, and freeing me from spent emotions. We played for a time in the grass, and then we sat quietly side by side.

"I am here to look at the lessons of that part of us that we call shadow," I explained, as he looked me expectantly.

"Let us away!" he said, and I climbed onto his back, grabbing the fur of his neck for balance as he bounded off. Time has no meaning in journeys, but after what seemed like a lifetime of flying through thick grasslands, the wind pelting my face briskly, we slowed as we approached a beach.

Hearing music and laughter, I looked toward the sound to see my ex-husband Mac, drink in hand, scuba gear leaning against a cooler. Surrounded by friends, he told story after story in his warm, captivating style;

the crowd gathered around him laughed and played. Always the life of the party, known affectionately as "Mr. Adorable," Mac could charm the pants off anyone alive. Anywhere he went, he immediately befriended everyone, turning any event into a wild party. I gazed upon his glowing face fondly. This was Mac at his very best. On his forearm, I could see his familiar tattoo of the Buddhist "om," his personal symbol of spiritual connection and oneness with all.

"I'm so jealous," I told the lion. "Why can't I play like that? Why do I have to be so responsible and hardworking? I want what he has!"

"Do you?" my guide purred.

Then everything changed. Now Mac was in a small dingy room, surrounded by elegant but dust-covered antiques inherited from his blue-blood family. His only remaining friend was the little dog at his side licking his face. He sat in his recliner alone, remote control in hand, watching television. He got up and opened the refrigerator to grab a cold beer and pop it open. Passing a mirror, he stopped and stared at his sallow yellow skin, telling the tale of liver fatigue. Lifting his tattooed arm to his face, he massaged his sore gums, where his teeth had been recently extracted. Sitting once again, he grabbed the remote and started to flip the channels, endlessly searching for something long lost.

A tear rolled down my cheek as I felt his despair. Then, suddenly, we were off again. The wind blew past my face as we headed to another place.

This time we found ourselves in a coffee bar full of energy. As we passed each group, close enough to hear the conversation, the chatter of voices congealed into bits of intellectual abstractions. In the background a live band played a soulful song, beckoning each of us to dig deep and uncover the juiciest parts of the deep passions of our lives.

My old friend Shelly was playing bass guitar. Though I had not seen her in a long, long time, she was as vibrant as ever. I knew that she was living on the road, stopping wherever she found herself at dusk, playing for her supper as the mood struck her. On the way to her table, she turned to the bartender and asked for a glass of wine. Dipping into a rich cheesy fondue, she licked her fingers and sipped the wine, quenching her immediate needs. Then she picked up her camera and cruised the smoky room, gathering images. After packing up her guitar, she waved good-bye and hit the road again.

"Oh, I hate this. I'm jealous again. I can feel it in my bones—my longing for freedom, the open road, for places and things unknown."

Again I felt us leaping through time. We stopped in a dark alley, where Shelly knocked twice on the door at the end. In the darkness I saw someone peek out. Envelopes exchanged. Shelly looked around furtively and made her way to a small room, where she poured the contents of the packet into a spoon, melting it over a candle flame and drawing it up into a dirty syringe lying on the small broken table. I looked away. The tiny cubicle was wallpapered with photographs, each one a glittering piece of art. The light and shadows danced on the glossy paper, creating stories and feelings that spoke louder than any words or song. I cried out, unheard, "Where is your family, Shelly? Your husband? Your home? Your cats? What did you do with your guitar? Did you even sell your camera this time? Oh, Shelly."

I clung to lion's fur with sadness as we bounded onward, and he reminded me that I had wanted to look at the shadow side of life. I heard drumming, just like the drumming that I had walked through to this journey, and asked him where we were headed.

"To another time, another memory, another friend."

The drumming quickened its pace as we arrived in a clearing where the dust was blowing up from the rhythmic stomping of people in spirit who were trance dancing, transported by the joy of the physical dance. Sage and tobacco smoke filled the air, and the people in a circle around the fire chanted in a language unknown to me.

Then I saw Bonnie, my dear friend, her face radiant with joyful belonging. Dressed in the cloth of the initiate, she chanted and danced in the middle of the circle, surrounded by her community. This was her night. She had trained hard, giving of herself freely, immersing herself in the teachings. Day and night she had worked—washing, assisting, cooking, and gathering. Having sacrificed all, the boundaries of her self had been effectively wiped away. She had truly ceased being the person that she had been before. She had arrived and now was one of her tribe.

"Oh, I am jealous of her belonging. I have never invested myself so completely in anything. I never leaped with such abandon, losing myself to that degree. I've never belonged like that!"

Then we traveled again to a room in the suburbs where Bonnie sat alone, blankly, surrounded by signs of her numb existence, rigidly filled with a hectic schedule of PTA meetings, baseball tournaments, dinners, and neighborhood events. The phone rang, but she let the voicemail take a message. Having lost herself so completely, she had run scared, not wanting to connect with anyone. Afraid to leap again to find her deep passion, she blocked it all out. Where was the glowing face, the ecstasy? Afraid of losing herself in belonging, she walled herself off, belonging to no one and no place.

Then once again I was sitting with my guide by the stream in the mountain meadow. "Lion! I wouldn't trade my life for theirs ever! Why was I jealous? What monstrous life situations! The brightness in each of their lives was overcome by their shadow sides. I am saddened and don't know what to make of what we saw."

Lion looked at me long and hard. "All the visions you had are about you, my friend. You have many such stories in your life. Never confuse them with truth. They are your stories. You can learn a great deal from them about the consequences of various actions and paths, and then choose your dreams with intent."

"What about my jealousy?"

"What is jealousy if not a form of inspiration?" he questioned. "Why would you create such long-lived stories if they were not about you? Aren't all the things you are jealous of also a part of you?"

"Does that mean that those shadow sides are part of me, too?" I asked him.

"Of course. If they weren't, those scenes would have had no emotional impact on you. That is your shamanic mirror. Listen to your feelings. Your heart speaks clearer than your mind, as long as you feel your feelings and don't think them. Your life story could have gone very differently. Imagine what other choices you could have made. Your longing to have fun and to be free could have led you to decide to have an abortion, to never have had children at all. Your love of play could have led you to succumb to drugs and alcohol, destroying your health, relationships, and work. Or you could have used your lack of a high school diploma and all of your responsibilities as a lifelong excuse to have others take care of you, and never tried to do anything on your own. Your wish to belong could have led you to submit to a guru, giving all your power away as an excuse to have another take responsibility for it. All those things are a part of you and have an impact on your life.

"The choices you have made have also had their shadow sides. You have surely made choices that brought unwanted consequences. At times, you have been afraid to leap into the unknown yet again. Once you glimpsed your dreams, can you really say that you have been consistent in energizing them again and again, honing and clarifying them with lessons learned from consequences? Have you leaped into each dream, adjusting by the moment until it became dynamically aligned with your soul?"

"I am afraid I have not been that courageous," I answered carefully. "I have blown through the circumstances of my life like a leaf in the wind, rarely allowing myself to dream my own dreams, to leap into the void, to fly. Looking honestly at my actions, at my choices, I have too often subjugated my wishes to take care of my responsibilities, while surfing the energy of others' dreams. That enabled me to avoid my shadow side, but along with it my jealousy grew, especially of those who I felt were afforded the opportunity to leap fully by my taking responsibility. I see now that this is just another story. A cop-out. Each time I was afraid to leap, I died in a sense. I have retrieved my soul; now I must take the next step and fly with it. When I take risks, my dreams are not static choices but dynamic ways of being."

As I spoke these words, the lion looked at me with a knowing smile on his wise old face. Then he gave me a playful but powerful nudge with his head, and I rolled into the cold water of the stream. I emerged, breathless and laughing, saying, "Yes, I understand that means living always in the present, taking risks, and coming to terms with my own shadow."

"Why is part of you shadow?" he asked. "Why do people love the pretty beauty of the butterfly of the daytime and abhor the striking beauty of the night's moth? Why is night bad and day good?"

His questions made me think of the beloved Africa of my childhood, and the African traditions that are deeply connected to the shadow, to the night. I have experienced their power. I felt my love for the energy of the African land, the energy of the senses, of the physical, of the dark, and I knew it could not be bad. I remembered the Shuar ways of honoring all energy and embracing the physical, Mother Earth.

Reading my thoughts, the lion said, "You are all of that, and you are learning to love and honor that part in all. So tell me, what makes shadow dangerous? Why do you fear it?"

I could feel in my heart what I wanted to articulate, but finding the words required translating these heart-based feelings into mind-based words. I stared at the stream while I formulated an answer. "It has great power. It can lead us into trouble, to places in life we don't want to find ourselves, to situations not aligned with our true dreams. Isn't that why we feel the shadow is evil?"

The lion answered, "But isn't it the very devaluing of shadow that makes it bad? Isn't it the reaction to these ways of being that creates the negative situations?"

I sat straight up with the force of recognition. "Yes! These sides of ourselves create actions and energize fantasies that are counter to our dreams when they are denied. The more they are seen as negative or bad, the more distorted they grow and the more trouble we find ourselves in. They become monsters, and when we act them out and give them energy in our lives, they create situations that are by definition unwanted and destructive. Yet we are our shadow sides as much as we are our self-described light."

I thought about how, in the life of each of the dear ones we had visited on our journey, shadow had a beneficial aspect that could have been life enhancing, if it had been aligned with the soul. Mac's magnetic personality, his storytelling ability, his passionate joie de vivre; Shelly's creativity, her deep intuitive nature, her huge heart; Bonnie's compassionate nature, her dedicated commitment, her generosity of self, her ability to invest herself in projects, communities, and traditions—each needed to be balanced by spirit and aligned with intent in order to blossom in ways that enhanced both self and community.

Then I thought about how our culture fears the shadow as bad or even evil. In the past that fear took the form of witch hunts—burning at the stake all that represents the pull of the earth-based existence called life, the goddess energies that honor the moon, the senses, and spirit in the physical. Through our distaste of shadow, we manifest fantasy and suffering.

I realized that each of us faces the challenge of embracing our shadow and defining all of ourselves—light and shadow—as useful, beautiful, and divine. I saw with new clarity that my dream is that we can embody all of our spirit and direct our energies with strong intent, aligned with our soul's purpose. We can individuate by building a strong sense of spirit and, at the same time, embrace our eternal oneness, investing fully in the community of all there is, ever was, and ever will be. As the shadow part of our communal being—long kept alive in indigenous shamanic communities worldwide—becomes part of our awareness once again, the ancient prophecy will materialize and "the eagle will again fly high with the condor."

I looked down and saw my paws large and firmly grounded. I had merged with the lion, and thus with playfulness and wisdom, sharp claws and big heart, freedom and responsibility. I lay down and began to lick my paws, cleaning myself lovingly with my tongue.

The drumbeat quickened. The call back had begun, and I returned to the room. Opening my eyes slowly, I allowed my awareness to return gently to my surroundings. We all sat up, wrapped in our insights and messages from the journey. John Perkins, shaman and shapeshifter, was drumming loudly to rouse us. He caught my eyes, smiling. I smiled back broadly and full of knowing joy.

Flexing the Shamanic Muscle

Shamanic training begins with a death—dying to old ways of perceiving—
and a leap into new eyes, new ways of perceiving reality. With new eyes to
see my dream in life, I began to rearrange my busy schedule in order to
accommodate this opportunity to follow my heart. At workshops I learned
techniques to access other realities and was introduced to more of my guides.
It is said that when the student is ready, the teacher appears. I am not sure
if this is true, but certainly teachers appeared before me everywhere I went.
I was asked by several shamans to return to Ecuador to apprentice. I also had
opportunities to study right in Baltimore, and then around the world. At first
I was reluctant—why me? Why a plastic surgeon? I had all the excuses—no
time, no money or aptitude, too much responsibility, too much debt. I tried
to avoid the inevitable, and still I was drawn. In the end I surrendered, and
as my studies continued, I longed for that one master, a guru, someone to
whom I could abdicate my will. But this was not to be my fate.

There were so many brilliant healers, holy people who lived in spirit in
so many differing ways. I learned from them all. In Baltimore I learned
much from Ipupiara (the Brazilian Amazonian shaman who met with my
first Dream Change study group before we embarked on our trip) and his
wife, Cleicha, an Andean shaman; from Wolf, an Iroquois healer; from
Running Water, a Taino curandero; from Ann Bell, a Reiki master; and so
many more. I went to India, to the Himalayas, to Africa. Everywhere I
went I met with more wisdom, with more teachers. Yet my search for that
one guru that would erase my personal responsibility eluded me.

One day—in answer to my request for help in finding the one master
teacher to whom I would succumb—two of my guides came to me in a
journey. A beautiful, flowing Earth woman and a gentle Christ-like man,
they carried a message:

"Spiritual power has long been something attainable only by the few,
often through years of study and deprivation. For most, connection to the
divine was sought only through intermediaries. In comparison, this age is
one of spiritual empowerment. It is a time of great change and remembrance—each one remembering our divine core, our individual connection,

our individual truth. Now is the time for us all to remember this and em-power ourselves spiritually. Go and speak this message. All are indigenous to this Mother Earth. Remind all of humanity of their indigenous nature, and of their responsibility to treat their Earth Mother and Cosmic Father in an honoring way, to develop their own spiritual connections, and to stop the endless search for the clarity and power that already lies within them."

With that understanding, I set forth to fulfill my promise to my guides. My connection with all my spirit guides and with the spirits of the world around me deepened, and I learned from them—from the wind, the clouds, the mountains, the trees, the rivers, the rocks, the birds. . . . After some time I realized that everything was my teacher, every object, person, and event. I came to see that there was no good or bad. Or perhaps you could say that it is all good, and all bad. I discovered that when I entered other realities, my guides were always with me to assist in gathering the information, energy, and power that I needed for the job at hand. Thus, as with all shamans, my training evolved at my own pace and style, set by my own intent and by the challenges that arose.

In the countless exhilarating hours of assisting various indigenous sha-mans in healing ceremonies, I learned rituals and tools to help focus and direct energy. As I spent more and more time at the homes of these sha-mans, I learned that journeying is not only an essential practice of shamanic work, but an integral part of life in shamanic communities. It is encour-aged, discussed at length within the extended family and community every day, and allowed to develop into a way of life. This way of being creates other realms in which to learn and grow, other realms in which to play and rehearse, other realms in which to live. These other realms and life experi-ences are not thought of as any less real or useful than the life and realm that we all commonly experience. Journeying is much more than personal fantasy. In fact, people will often journey together, and these are shared life experi-ences in much the same way that daytime events are.

In the workshops that I attended, I discovered that journeying is a natural capacity that all human beings have. Those of us who have grown up in non-shamanic cultures are just a little out of practice. In our culture, young children have much more freedom to daydream and fantasize than older children and adults, for whom this is strictly curtailed as wasteful and nonsensical. Some of us even had imaginary friends as childhood companions, our daydreams taking the form of humans or animals that we interacted with in the same way that we interacted with our families and other friends. Whether or not our waking dreams took the form of imaginary friends, most of us journeyed with ease and frequency when we were very young. However, at some point as we grew older, this practice was discouraged and effectively squashed. We still have the natural capacity; it just hasn't been used for a very long time. We have not flexed this muscle, and it has atrophied. But I was amazed to see how quickly the muscle responds once activated again, even in very skeptical individuals.

Journeying is an extension of dreaming. No one taught us how to dream, yet we all have vivid dreams. Dreams often present themselves to us in bizarre forms, and they are full of images, sensations, and feelings. They also give us information and messages. They lend assistance for our daytime life path, with all its follies, turmoil, and decisions, even when we are not consciously aware of the impact that they are having on us or do not remember them when we awaken. Dreams are also asking something from us. They are in part calls to attention. This is what a psychotherapist might say, and these notions have been extensively researched and applied by generations of medical and psychotherapeutic practitioners. Dreams are also a way to access information, power, and energy.

I learned that just as every dream is different and we each have our own way of dreaming, every journey is different, and everyone accesses their power and energy in their own way. Some journeys are very sensory—vividly visual or auditory or focused on touch, smell, or taste. A journey can be primarily emotional or primarily informational, or a combination of sensation, emotion, and ideas. Some journeys are very fast, others slow; some symbolic, others straightforward; some instantaneous and short, others long and drawn out. None of this matters. Over the years, I noticed that people settle into a way of journeying that works best for them. Often the people who initially had the most difficult time with journeying—who became the most frustrated listening to others' descriptions of journeys while they felt they were not experiencing anything—were the ones who later became the most able to experience journeying and apply it to their lives.

As I made regular journey practice a part of my life, I developed a mutually trusting relationship with the process (often in the form of guides, but not always). I discovered that the method that best fits the time allowed and the situation—even the boardroom or the operating room—presents itself. I found that the more I began to use it, the more I flexed this muscle, the more it worked. And that's the bottom line. Shamanic practice works.

I initially performed healings with my dear friend and colleague Elizabeth Kramer, and then I began performing countless individual healings on my own. I continue training every day and every night, in every situation, in every event, in every feeling, in every relationship, in every sensation. In fact, it is almost impossible to say exactly when my shamanic training began. When did yours? Hasn't everything that we have learned through our life path led us to today, giving us useful tools and ways of being? Is our very life our training? Is there training before this life? After? Simultaneous to this physical reality? I do not mean to say that I know the answer to these questions, but I am open to the possibilities. Knowing the "answer" or the "truth" according to the perspective of our current reality may not, in fact, be a practical goal if it closes us to further learning.

I trained as a trip facilitator for Dream Change Coalition and began to take people on my own to experience these magical transformational experiences. I visited the shamans in South America several times a year, and they, in turn, began to visit me at my home in the United States, where we worked together for weeks at a time.

Thus I lived with one foot in two worlds. It was a trying experience. I remember one time when I had cleared my schedule to be with Esteban Tamayo at my home, and we had a day of about thirty healings set up. Halfway through the day I got a call with the news that one of my patients had fallen accidentally, injuring her recent breast implants and causing bleeding. I had to rush in, prepare the operating room, and drain the hematoma. The abrupt shift from healings performed with chanting, feathers, stones, and eggs to scrubbing up in the operating room was startling, but I found that in the process I was more closely connected to my guides. As a result I was able to complete the operation much more quickly and successfully.

I have known many who have dealt with these opposing worldviews by abandoning everything familiar and surrendering themselves to foreign lifestyles, forgoing former family members, relationships, and possessions. Although for some it seems to be the only way to proceed with integrity, my teachers of the Andes and Amazon often find this hard to comprehend. They see it as a ridiculous dishonoring of Mother Earth, family, spirit, and our ancestors.

I have been fortunate to find a way to integrate both paths of healing in my life. I have continued to maintain my busy surgical practice and active devotion to my children and grandchildren. When my daughter Alice was near to term with her second child, my dear friend and powerful shaman Maria Juana Yamberla gave invaluable aid. Her hands-on assistance allowed Alice's mind and body to relax deeply, freeing up energy for her womb to begin its important work of contractions.

Shungo—From My Heart to Yours

As Maria Juana worked with Alice, I remembered assisting her in a healing at her home in Ecuador. Although very short in physical stature, Maria has a gentle power that creates an enormous presence. Her emotions are always right on the surface—it seems she is always laughing, crying, or hugging and kissing. A beautiful and devout woman, she is known far and wide for her healing powers. She frequently calls on her spirit guides Jesus and Mary in her shamanic healing rituals. A steady stream of patients finds its way to her door high in the Andes Mountains.

Maria Juana works with her husband, Antonio. Her training began in utero when her father heard her call out in the womb and knew she was a shaman. Antonio's started after they were married and she began to train him. When the two shamans—teacher and student, wife and husband— work together, she does the spiritual work at her altar. Through chanting and prayer she communicates with spirit, and—assisted by her favorite spirit guide, the white dove—she reads the patient's energy from a candle that has been rubbed over the body. In trance she obtains information, energy, and power. Her altar is covered with huacas, sacred stones from the surrounding volcanoes, which she feeds frequently by camaying them with trago, sacred sugarcane alcohol.

Camaying is an age-old technique used in healing traditions. The word is difficult to translate; it is always a challenge to explain concepts that are beyond our concise physical view of the world. It can be loosely translated as blowing spirit, sharing connection.

As Maria Juana camays at her altar, Antonio simultaneously camays the patient with trago, cinnamon, powdered Amazonian seedpods, and cologne. Antonio then rhythmically urticates* the patient with nettles and other healing plants and cleanses their energy fields using eggs, all the while chanting and invoking spirit's assistance. Maria Juana at her corner altar goes in and out of trance, directing Antonio to pay attention here, spend more time cleansing there.

This time I had arrived with a group of ten on a Dream Change Coalition trip that I was facilitating. A woman stood stark naked in front of the rest of our group in the center of the healing space, a small adobe room with the altar and benches along the walls. Maria Juana insists that healings be done in the nude, especially with us from the North. Through the years she has noticed that we are surprisingly "hung up" on our bodies, and she finds that releasing this through being healed in the nude is an important step in removing blockages so that our body's energy can flow more freely. It is also better for us, because after being camayed and getting wet in the cold Andean air, we have something dry to put back on.

The young woman had asked for a healing because, despite years of

---

*To *urticate* means to raise welts on the skin by brushing, or "flogging," the body with stinging nettle plants. The Latin name for the nettle plant family is Urticaceae. Although this prickly plant is considered a weed in many areas, it has traditionally been used in teas and herbal remedies worldwide. Urtication has been used as a healing practice for millennia and was described as being in common usage around the time of Jesus Christ. It is still used today in some circles, notably in the treatment of arthritis.

medical treatments, she had not been able to become pregnant. Maria Juana worked steadily while Antonio camayed. She made a pendulum out of carnations and used this over the patient's candle. She also filled a cup with orange soda pop, infusing her spirit into the drink through prayer, camaying, and plopping in selected huacas. At the same time she made a "doll" out of cookies, infusing them with spiritual connection and healing energy. In some cases, after Antonio is finished, and after he places the carnation necklace around the neck of the patient, patting the flowers onto the area of the heart, saying, "Shungo," Maria Juana takes over with more direct physical healing.*

On that day Maria Juana led the woman to a blanket. There, with the patient lying on the floor, the shaman used her hands to adjust "the mother," the womb, the source of a woman's creative powers. She manipulated the uterus in the pelvic floor by deeply probing the abdomen with her gentle but strong fingers. I assisted in the healing by lifting the woman up and down, yelling, "Shungo, Shungo!" and shaking her to help release the stuck energy. When "the mother" loosened and dropped into good position, Maria Juana was satisfied and beckoned the woman to stand up. I led her back to the bench to begin getting dressed. Maria Juana handed me the orange soda and cookies, mixed with some of the flower petals. She almost always has her patients eat and drink this as part of their healing to connect their bodies to her and to her spirit guides.

Maria Juana then studied the candle to see the effectiveness of the healing.

"You have just finished your period," she told, rather than asked, the woman.

"Yes, that is correct."

"You will not have another one until after the birth of your son in ten months," she stated matter-of-factly.

During the following months, I watched this beautiful woman through

---

Shungo is another Quechua word with no good translation. A short definition would be "from my heart to yours" or—like the salutations *namaste* and *aloha*—"we are all one; my divinity recognizes the divinity in you."

the process of her pregnancy and the birth of her perfect baby boy. She shapeshifted her energy and became a mother in every way.

I have seen Maria Juana and Antonio heal in this way—with food, herbs, and manipulation, through prayer, physical touch, and connection—on numerous occasions. I have seen endometriosis cured, ovarian cysts and tumors removed. Maria Juana likes to treat female reproductive problems. Both her parents were "midwives," and she is particularly fond of and powerful in this arena. But it wouldn't be fair to stop there, for I have seen her cure with men, too—stomach cancer, back problems, addictions, and so on.

Like my mother, I am an empiricist at heart. But I cannot explain these healings in biochemical or pharmaceutical terms alone. The very fact that the effectiveness of shamanic healing is not completely explainable by our scientific view of the world gives us a clue that an important breakthrough in our knowledge and understanding is possible. The shamans will tell you that faith is a prerequisite to true healing. It is much more difficult to align our dreams with intent without faith. Is faith something that can be instilled in or taught to someone else? I recall the words of Alberto Tatzo: "Faith is not the same as belief. Belief implies the lack of personal experience, the lack of knowing. True faith can grow only through knowledge born of our personal experience. Opening oneself to the possibility is the essential condition from which faith is born."

My study with shaman healers has been ongoing through many years over many continents. Each shaman has his or her own style of working, way of connecting to spirit, and personal techniques; I found that I learned something from each encounter, from the shaman human, and from the shaman spirit, from my own connection and questioning my guides. Much of my training has occurred in Ecuador with the Quechua, the Yachaks—birdpeople shamans of the Andes—and with the Shuar of the Amazon. I discovered that training in shamanic technique varies from culture to culture, area to area, and from person to person, yet the similarities are greater than the differences. Shamans share strikingly similar tools and techniques worldwide, whether they are in Ladakh or "Little Tibet," in North, South, or Central America, or in Africa. Among my fondest memories are the enlightening times spent both in the Andes and in the United States with the elders don Esteban Tamayo, Jose Joaquin Pineda, and Maria Juana Yamberla, and their families.

Taita Yachak—Master Shaman

Esteban Tamayo lives high in the Ecuadorian Andes, in the Valley of the Dawn. Don Esteban is a farmer in the sleepy town of Carabuela, Ecuador, near the town of Otavalo, about an hour north of the capital, Quito. The Otavalans are a highly sensual, beautiful, close-knit communal people, their native dress identifying them around the world. The women wear dark woolen wraparound skirts with blousy white embroidered tops, bejeweled with layer after layer of gold and coral necklaces, bracelets, and earrings. The men typically dress in white short pants, white shirts, and deep blue ponchos, their heads covered with felt hats. Both men and women keep their hair long and braided, and their feet covered only with thin espadrilles in the cool Andean climate. Known worldwide for their weaving and knitting, the Otavalans sell clothing that is highly prized from Paris to Milan to New York. They are also known for their music, and in any Andean band there is likely to be an Otavalan. I knew them for their passion, their soul, their dedication, their honor.

Don Esteban is a healer shaman in the Incan tradition. His shamanic powers having become apparent while he was still in his mother's womb, he went on to learn many of his skills from his mother. Five decades later he has taught his two sons, Jose and Jorge, and together they form a formidable force of shamanic healing power, each one adding his unique talents and energies in healing ceremonies.

The Tamayos remain deeply connected to their homeland and to their people, the Quechua. Indigenous people who live in very much the same way as they have for millennia, the Quechua of Ecuador are linguistically and culturally connected with other Quechua-speaking people throughout the Andes, from Colombia to Bolivia. In fact, there are almost as many Quechua-speaking as Spanish-speaking people in Ecuador. The Yachaks

Above: Eve's parents Marvin Weinstein, Ph.D., and Fay Weinstein, M.D.

Right: Eve at age 13 with a cheetah in Kenya.

Below: Eve took this photo of her brother Benny when they were children growing up in Africa.

Above: Yachak shaman Alberto Tatzo with Dream Change Coalition leader John Perkins in Ecuador.

Below: Shaman Alberto Tatzo performing a healing at his home in the Andes.

Above: Yachak
Birdperson shaman
Maria Juana Yamberla
in her healing room
near Otavalo, Ecuador
in the Andes.

Right: Eve blowing fire
onstage at a workshop
conducted at the
University of Michigan
Medical School.

Right: Don Esteban Tamayo, Yachak Birdperson shaman, arranging items on his alter in preparation for a healing ceremony near Otavalo, Ecuador.

Below: Eve, Pedro, and shaman don Esteban after the baptism of Esteban's grandson, (Eve's godson and Pedro's son) Edwin, at don Esteban's house near Otavalo.

Above: Shaman Antonio (Maria's husband), Eve's son Jock, shaman Maria Juana Yamberla, Eve's daughter Coale, Eve, and Eve's granddaughter Blake, at Eve's home in Baltimore.

Below: Eve and her family.

Above: Shuar Juan Arcos (Peem) and Eve on bridge in Miazal, Shuar territory, Ecuador.

Right: Eve playing the Tumank, a Shuar instrument, Miazal.

Below: Eve with Maria Rosa Shakai, Mariano Chumpi, and their children in Miazal, Upper Amazon, Ecuador.

Left: Eve in Miazal, Ecuadorian Amazon.

Middle: Airstrip in the Amazon, Miazal, Ecuador, where Dream Change Coalition takes trips (no electricity, no roads).

Below: Shuar Shaman Daniel Wachapa in Detroit, Michigan for a gathering of shamans. Photo by Tom Knoll.

*Above: Eve at Lamayury
Monastary in Ladakh,
India.*

*Right: Eve with Ladakhi
Oracle, Leh, Ladakh.*

*Below: Crowd of lamas
watching at Wesak Festival
with Dalai Lama, Leh,
Ladakh.*

are the healers of their communities, using techniques handed down through the ages—from the time of the Incan Empire and before. A steady flow of visitors arrives at the homes of the Tamayos to be healed—from the community and from all over the world. Stories of their shamanic skill and power have spread far and wide, and in recent years we have been blessed with their willingness to teach outsiders in the fulfillment of the ancient Incan prophecy that in this new era "the eagle will fly with the condor" in harmony. Married in sacred ceremony to the mountains, to the land and the sacred waters, they access this powerful connection on their journeys.

I met Esteban Tamayo on my first trip to Ecuador. During that first transformational trip, I saw and experienced the incredible power of this gentle and humble man. He is short in stature, as is the case with all the Quechua people, so at first glance one might see an unimposing, quiet old man. Closer up, however, as with Maria Juana, his energy and power create a towering presence. Yet his energy and power are very different from that of Maria Juana. At once gentle and fierce, joking and sincere, probing and distant, he is a master of the forces of nature, and of connecting simultaneously with spirit and physical presence. Fire is the element with which he works most closely, becoming one with the volcanoes and camaying fire with formidable and overwhelming strength. His healings go deep to the core with potent cleansing and infusing energy.

I had been studying under don Esteban and his two sons ever since that first awe-inspiring meeting in the Andes of Ecuador. After three years of study, along with my close friend, Elizabeth Kramer, a Peruvian-American acupuncturist, I was ready for initiation into the circle of Yachaks. Don Esteban would lead us to the sacred springs for the initiation ceremony—our "marriage to the volcanoes."

Entering the Circle of Yachaks

Father Sun, Inti, rose over Imbabura as it has done since the time of the Incas, and before. I arose filled with emotions—excitement, anticipation, love, honor. The fiery warmth burned into my face, while the brisk cold wind caressed my body, the dust encircling my nostrils, the dew underfoot. This was to be the day of my initiation. I was entering the circle of Yachaks, birdpeople shamans of the high Andes.

Initiation. The Penguin dictionary describes it: "To initiate is to bring one in." At the same time, it has the meaning of the Greek word *teleutan*, "to die.". . . It was a good day to die.

I had seen many people die. Death and disease were frequent companions in medical school and residency, where I had been through rigorous training. When I finished the program, I was the first and only woman to have successfully completed training at the Saint Agnes Hospital surgical residency program in Baltimore, a program that started in 1906. I had survived seven years of surgical residency, with its forty-hour shifts, its continual tests of endurance, its harsh demands that required me to think and act rapidly, making lifesaving decisions without the time to reflect and weigh the options. Yes, I had been through initiations before. This one was different.

After rising early with the sun, Elizabeth and I set off to gather supplies. We would be making offerings to the sacred springs, demonstrating our deep respect. As we walked along the street in the cold morning air, my dear friend Shruthi Mahalingaiah approached. A native of India, a medical student at Harvard, and a student of shamanism, she had come to be witness for Elizabeth and me. Once we were ready, we set off for Taita (master teacher) don Esteban's home, where we would join don Esteban, Jorge, and Jose for the hour-long hike to the springs.

The six of us walked the long country path, carrying our offerings of trago, red roses, wine, tobacco, chicken, and rice. Looking out over the valley, I saw the smoke from a cooking fire rise through the air. Over to the left I caught sight of a woman working the land. She was heavily pregnant, a toddler playing at her feet. Jorge and I walked together.

"How are your children?" he asked sincerely. He and his father and brother had spent time at my home with my family. We had all become very close and considered each other's families as our own.

"Alice is pregnant again," I said, catching up on news.

"Abuelita [little grandmother]!" he exclaimed, "Your second grandchild!

You were a very young mother. Today, *abuela*, we will ceremonially connect with this valley. In the same way that we are connected to our human families, this land will also be your family."

We walked along dry, barren fields, passing an old Incan ruin before descending into the valley. Onward we trekked, single file, up hills, down canyons, and across rivers. Whenever I have been in Ecuador, I have felt that the entire country is a power place. Because it is on the equator, it is spinning faster than countries at other latitudes. The mountains of Ecuador are the farthest from the center of the earth—even farther than Everest—and the closest to the sun. It is said that the Incas, sun worshippers, conquered Ecuador to be closer to the sun; because of the natural topography, it was not necessary to erect temples there.

The valley along which we hiked is known to be a particularly powerful and sacred place, a vortex of power formed by three volcanoes, the male Imbabura and his two female consorts, Cotocachi and Mojanda. The energy is staggering. There are more than sixty shamans in the valley, and they regard the springs where our initiation ceremonies would be held with both reverence and fear. We had heard that fifteen people had successfully been through initiation ceremonies there, and eight others had died in the attempt.

Some time later, back in the United States, I was asked if I had been afraid that day. Reflecting back, I realized that I was not. I had total trust in my teachers, and I was prepared to die physically if that was to be. However, I did remember another time when I had been in Otavalo, attending the baptismal fiesta of don Esteban's grandson Joel. I had been handed a microphone and asked to sing in front of the entire village, and then I was scared out of my wits. But on the day of initiation I was not afraid, not even of dying.

As we hiked along, Shruthi talked of her great frustration in medical school. "Here I am, on a hill in the valley between three powerful volcanoes. I can feel the power; I know the power. I have spent a year studying with shamans in the rainforests, mountains, and islands in Ecuador and Bali. I have seen and experienced much that I would have considered miracles before. I have come to see the world around me in a new way, to be aware of subtle energy fields that I was oblivious to before—to commune with nature, with spirit, and to truly receive the messages, the knowledge, the gifts. Yet in medical school, there is so much emphasis on scientific method, on proofs, on control. Sometimes I get frustrated and confused. Many of the things that I have learned cannot be seen without faith. If you need to have 'proof' before something is visible, it will never be seen!"

"I know exactly what you mean," I answered, as we continued along the path. "Do not despair, but rather remember how very blessed we have been to experience and learn both ways of being, both ways of healing. Do you agree, Elizabeth?" I asked. "Have you found practicing acupuncture and Chinese medicine while trying to integrate native North and South American as well as Indian traditions to be frustrating?"

"At times, especially at first," she answered, "but with so many methods of diagnosis and treatment at my disposal, I find that I can help people in very profound ways. It is no coincidence that the three of us—representing many ancestral cultures and traditions in ourselves—are here together to-day," she continued. "We, as well as the global community, will be well served by bridging these cultures."

We talked about the need to bridge the many ways of viewing health, of viewing disease, of viewing death, of viewing the world around us.

"It seems each of us has witnessed this in a very powerful way," Shruthi said, "and we have also seen that when bridges are not formed, serious collisions occur."

"Yes," I replied, "instead of lamenting this or giving up, we can look at cultural collisions and the interfaces of differing realities as opportunities for advancing knowledge. Each one gives us a fresh opportunity to leap to new ways of understanding and new ways of viewing the world around us."

As we approached the sacred spring, we could hear a pounding beat—"tun, tun, tun"—a pulse, the heartbeat of Pachamama. Pachamama, a Quechua term for Mother Earth, means far more than our culture's understanding of the term. How can we begin to understand when the words for translation don't exist in our languages, and the concepts are not a part of our lives or of our view of the world around us? The closest we can come is by bracketing concepts and conceiving of them as an unbroken whole: earth/ universe/time—the space-time continuum.

Although it had been cold at the beginning of our trek, we had been hiking for some time with heavy loads, and the heat of the noonday sun was overwhelming. Feeling sticky and dizzy in the heat, I was reminded of the jungle, and of my other teachers, the Shuar. "Tun, tun, tun"—we were close. In the sweltering heat we got on our hands and knees and crawled through brambles and thorn bushes. I felt just like I imagined a baby would feel pushing its way through the birth canal. We were closer still. The sound reverberated—"tun, tun, tun"—deafening in its intensity. Arriving at the spring, we laid down our bundles and took it all in. Noxious fumes prickled our nostrils. We sat and rested, each deep in our personal thoughts and prayers. I took a moment to recall those who had died a complete death, leaving their earthly bodies behind, and those who had been initiated, who had died by passing through the portal into a new way of being. Which was to be my fate today? I thought of my children at home, and of my beautiful granddaughter, and sent them a prayer.

I also thought of my mother, bedridden at home in Hawaii. I thought of her life as a physician, in which she was always ready to consider all methods for healing, even unconventional ones. A ferocious reader, a keen intellect, a hardy workhorse her entire life, she was suffering the ironic indignity of senility and stroke. Stuck in a state that was neither death nor life as she had envisioned it, she would have been frustrated and despairing had she been lucid.

Although I was still breathing heavily from the long trek, I noticed that my aging teacher, don Esteban, was already up again, singing and chanting to the spirits of the springs. The feeling of ecstasy that began to clothe my very being was a feeling akin to being home. I was home again.

One by one the group prepared to enter the cave from where the volcanic spring arose, the entrance and the small cave itself a close fit for even one person. Feeling the sun on my face, the blood coursing through my tired legs, the beat of my heart and the beat of the earth connecting, I entered a place where time and space were continuous and eternal. Hearing my name called, as if through a tunnel, I stood and collected my offerings.

Still in trance I walked through the blood-red running waters and crawled on my knees to the entrance of the cave. The sound at the mouth of the cave was deafening, and the water pouring through was strong. Holding fast and gripping the rocks with my feet and elbows to keep myself from being knocked over, I made my way slowly into the cave, all the while cradling the food, wine, coins, and flowers in my arms.

Suddenly I was beyond the falls, and the noise ceased. A quiet, welcoming calm crept through my senses to the core of my being. Ceremonially making my offerings, I prayed to Pachamama, to the volcanoes, and to the sacred water. Then I was completely overcome—I curled up and lay down in the wet close space, like a baby once again in the womb. I have no concept of how long I lay there, for I know that I could have just stayed there forever with great pleasure, having melted into the earth, at one with the cave and simultaneously at one with all that is now, with all that ever was, and with all that ever will be.

In the end I again heard my name called from outside the cave. It was don Esteban letting me know that it was time to come forth into the world again, time to begin my life anew, time to initiate the dreams of the world. Initiation is not—as some believe—a graduation, an end. Initiation is truly a beginning of a new life, a new way of being. In that moment I sensed that I was crossing the threshold of a gateway leading to another life—one in which I would have much to learn and much to teach—and I fully accepted the responsibilities.

That day I was home. I am home. Wherever I am, I am at home with Pachamama in all her glory. We travel to find sacred places and power spots, but unless we realize our connection, we cannot find lasting tranquility. The one comment that is echoed again and again by participants on Dream Change Coalition trips is that they experienced a long-lasting connection to Pachamama, to Mother Earth, to the universe, to time, and to spirit—a connection that was lacking in their lives before.

My initiation deepened that connection through a ceremonial marriage, literally, to the land, to the volcanoes, to the sacred springs, to the spirits of the valley—to the path of the shaman.

6

Cultural Collisions

THE GROUND WAS A LONG WAY BELOW ME, and we were flying so fast that it was difficult to make out the terrain. We dipped down, and I could see a desert of sand and dunes, scattered with occasional shrub and thorn trees. On and on we flew. Finally the desert shrubbery coalesced into an oasis. As we neared I noticed pavement and buildings—a city of brick and mortar, a man-made landscape.

Then I saw it—the bed in the middle of the pavement. Someone was holding a clipboard at the foot of the bed, speaking to the patient who waned in pallor and pain. As we flew closer, I could make out the features of the white-coated person at the foot of the bed. It was me! I watched as my doctor persona took and carefully documented the pulse, blood pressure, and temperature of the patient, then pulled out a stethoscope to listen to the heart and lungs, and finally manually palpated the patient's tender belly. I saw myself begin to speak to the patient, but I could not make out the words.

I looked at my hands and noticed that they were grasping black feathers. I was flying on the back of a crow. The crow climbed higher. I thrilled to the exhilaration of the height and the wind on my face, my mind sensing rather than thinking. My heart filled with loving compassion.

Again the crow dove down. This time the terrain was dramatically different. Snowcapped peaks rose majestically along the horizon. I could hear a waterfall. Then I saw them. The sacred springs. The mist sprayed my face as we approached. People were singing and chanting ecstatically in the waters, laughing and praying. We landed on the hill nearby, and I watched as the group of people spoke to the waters and to the mountain. Searching the group, I saw myself once again, this time without clipboard, stethoscope, or white coat; instead I was fondling a stone lovingly with my fingers. I began to rub the stone over the woman standing in front of me, chanting all the while, connecting with and asking for assistance from spirit and from the elements surrounding and within us. After watching myself work on the patient with leafy branches and eggs, I climbed back on the crow and took off again. A strong sense of wholeness flowed through my consciousness, imbuing me with energy and power.

Fighting the Language Barrier

I was now a member of the circle of Yachaks, the Incan birdpeople shamans. I had been trained by shamans from the high Andes and Amazonia; from North, Central, and South America; from Africa and Asia. I was performing shamanic healings in which I incorporated Incan techniques with others that I had learned throughout the world and from my inner guides.

I was also an M.D., a plastic surgeon, a Fellow of the American College of Surgeons, a member of the American Society of Plastic Surgeons (ASPS), and a member of the prestigious American Society of Aesthetic Plastic Surgery (ASAPS). I was at the pinnacle of my field, with a busy private practice and my own outpatient operating facility.

I was now both of these—M.D. and shaman. How could I integrate the two? How could such seemingly disparate views of the world of healing, two completely crossed cultures, function together?

Many studies have been done on cross-cultural medicine. When healers who follow one set of healing customs and beliefs encounter patients of another, problems arise. Anne Fadiman writes of such problems in her book

The Spirit Catches You and You Fall Down: A Hmong Child, Her American Doctors, and the Collision of Two Cultures. The collision she describes is very painful and very real. Reading her book, I was reminded of a patient whom I took care of when I was a general surgery resident in the cardiac intensive care unit at Johns Hopkins Hospital in Baltimore. As a visiting third-year surgical resident, I was responsible for the pre- and postoperative critical care of all patients undergoing cardiac surgery. My job was one of "fine-tuning" their medications and care. Like the other residents, I was working forty-eight-hour shifts, with only ten hours of break time in each shift for eating and sleeping. My day began with 4:00 A.M. "pre-rounds" to assess all the patients and collect data before the 6:00 A.M. rounds with the cardiac surgery residents, who would then head off to the operating room to perform the operations.

Providing critical care was a grueling and thankless task. The patients in the unit would either sail smoothly through their postoperative course or "crash and burn" so suddenly it would make our heads spin. These moments of terror taught us to remain absolutely calm in the face of life-or-death situations, to think fast—even when exhausted from sleep deprivation—and to change course on a dime, reassessing and changing again until stabilization was reached.

The patient that I recalled was a gypsy "king." He was not one of the musicians in the popular band of that name but a true patriarch of a large gypsy clan. He had a failing heart and was scheduled for the most complex and arduous operation in cardiac surgery—a triple valve replacement. While we were preparing him for surgery with multiple invasive lines—a catheter into his bladder and arterial IV lines carefully placed to enable us to accurately and continuously monitor his blood composition and pressure—we got a glimpse of just such a cultural collision. Gypsies by the dozens, two by two, filed into his small cubicle. Once there, they would each kiss his feet, wail sorrowfully, and—as the nurses who were trying to get their work done bemoaned—"generally make a spectacle of themselves."

Informed consent was obtained for the operation, and I quickly saw that this strained the definition of both "informed" and "consent." What exactly is "informed consent" anyway? Even when someone has gone to medical school, specialized in the field in question, and performed the proposed procedure, can he or she really understand all the possible risks in personal terms? After the gypsy patriarch was prepared for surgery, one of his many sons came over to the team of nurses and residents who were responsible for his care. In a cold, calculating voice he informed us that he had a shotgun outside, and that he would not hesitate to use it if his father didn't make it out of the hospital alive and well.

Over the next few weeks this king of the gypsies took up all of our waking—and even our very coveted and diminutive sleeping—hours. At first he did very well, and the clan filing through would bring him gifts, sing him songs, rub his skin with sweet-smelling balms, and venerate his presence as best they could in a small crowded cubicle with someone on a ventilator and with plastic tubes in every orifice. Then his condition worsened. When he "crashed," he was rapidly stabilized, and new medications were added to his regimen. For several days we monitored his condition closely, titrating the medication dosages and adjusting regimens every five or ten minutes on a continual basis. But even with all of our efforts, his body deteriorated and his organ systems began to fail. He was dying.

His family and relatives were oblivious to his deterioration, continuing to bring gifts and praises day and night. No matter what the attending physicians said, they couldn't seem to communicate across the vast cultural chasm. In their world, he would not have had an operation. The functioning of his heart would have simply deteriorated, and his activities and appetites would have slowly decreased until he died. Without having any knowledge of the reasoning behind each step we were taking to care for him, how could they possibly understand that he could walk in well and leave dead? Or that the condition of his heart predicted certain death without the operation, and that this made it worth the risk? It was completely impossible for the family, with their view of the healing arts, to understand why he was still on life support. They came through the cubicle hourly, demanding that the tubes be removed, that he be taken off the ventilator, that he be given something to eat. The family would not accept that his physical demise was imminent.

In their world, healing is done gently, slowly, with plant medicine and prayer to help, and whatever the outcome, it unfolds clearly and slowly, with many signals—physical, emotional, mental, and spiritual—that let everyone know the probable direction. In the world of the intensive care unit, nothing is clear, nothing is gentle, and the signals as to the direction of the outcome are complex and technical, readable only by those trained to do so.

And I was one who was trained to do so. At the time I was so immersed in the second-by-second fine-tuning of the signals that we read so carefully and accurately that I had neither time nor energy to read the whole person, to feel the signals of his soul and those of his community.

I remember vividly when he died. It was late at night, and there were no family members with him. I was terrified to go out and tell the son and the rest of the family, and I frantically made calls to the attending physician's office, to hospital security and social workers, to the ministry—looking for anyone who could lend me support. I was terrified of the consequences of communicating the finality of his death to the family, terrified of the cultural clash that would surely occur in this otherwise well-controlled intensive care unit.

At that time of the night, there was no one who could come right away. I tentatively made my way into the waiting room and found the oldest son, the man who did not want to know that he was now the patriarch. I sat next to him, and he saw what I had to tell him in my eyes and body even before I spoke. Side by side we sat a minute, finally connecting on a deeper level, heart to heart, and I began to explain. Although the son did not follow through with his threat to bring a shotgun inside, his grief was painful to see. The wailing and writhing of the swelling number of gypsies is something I shall never forget.

As the years went by, I experienced many more cultural collisions, and I slowly began to see that this "collision of cultures" is very much a part of almost every patient-doctor interaction, taking its toll on doctors and patients alike. We don't usually take into account the fact that doctors and their patients come from very different cultures and very different realities.

They operate from very different assumptions and understandings about the workings of the human body and of life and death. Western medicine has become a culture all its own, indicated by the difference in language. In medical school I was frequently puzzled by colloquial terms for illnesses. What is "walking pneumonia"? As doctors, we had our own language. We would rattle off terms relating to the diagnoses, tests, and procedures that we were performing or had in mind. We named conditions and responses in a way that implied we had arrived at the *truth*. What we had actually done was make a long line of guesses based on the information available at the time, which we used to make more guesses about the next most valuable piece of information to be obtained on the path to "diagnosis" and "treatment." Intelligent guesses perhaps—even algorithms designed by brilliant people in the field and based on thousands of similar events with like symptoms, physical findings, and data—yet still guesses. I came to realize that in medical practice, just as in physics, truth is a relative term that has meaning only in relationship to the observer's reality.

On another occasion, a close friend, Linda, an extremely intelligent, educated, and competent healer, told me about taking her son to his pediatrician. She fumed as she told me the story. One day her son was wheezing and having difficulty breathing, so she took him to the pediatrician to be checked. She mentioned that she had felt that she had a good rapport with the doctor, and that he was competent and caring. But then she burst out, "The doctor told me he had asthma. How could he say that! I got so angry with him. He shouldn't use words like that. I asked him to just tell me what was going on with my son in descriptive terms." When I countered that asthma *is* a descriptive term, this gentle compassionate mother became furious: "Words have meaning. Bad connotations. Asthma has a lot connected with it." She couldn't even begin to consider that the doctor was just trying to do his job, the best he could, within the limits of his training, the available tools, and his view of disease. Her reactions made me realize that the terms doctors use to give a diagnosis may often be heard by the patient not as a description but as a sentence.

Bridging Two Worlds

Now, having become a shaman, I faced an internal cultural collision. I had been trained in two very divergent ways of healing, two very different ways of looking at disease, at the body, and at the world. One day I discussed these contrasting traditions with Esteban Tamayo and his shaman son Jorge.

"Taita Yachak," I queried, with Jorge translating, "in medical school we were taught rules and principles; we memorized huge quantities of data, as well as learned where to look up things in books when we need to access information that we have forgotten. This has not been the case with my shamanic training, which occurs moment by moment through spirit. And diagnosis—that's something else. I'm not sure what my medical school teachers would say if I told them I was diagnosing with the use of a simple candle!"

"Yes, we do things in a completely different way from the hospitals," don Esteban explained. "In a shamanic healing the diagnosis is done by sensing the spirit of the person through intuitive means, accessing information from the spiritual realm, and using varying techniques to focus. We begin with the assumption that all disease has a spiritual basis, so we use methods such as chanting and prayer, invoking the help of the spirit world, traveling to the spiritual realm to effect change there, gathering information and power, and even bringing back soul parts from the spiritual realm to the physical. Only after the spiritual basis is addressed and any blockages to the flow of energy are removed does the shaman address the physical, emotional, and mental bodies by making prescriptions as to behavior, manipulations, and herbal and nutritional remedies."

As I listened to him, it became clearer to me than ever before that allopathic medicine and shamanic healing have two completely different starting points. Allopathic medicine starts with the Cartesian assumption that our physical bodies are separate from our spiritual bodies and thus attempts to heal with purely physical methods, such as physical and chemical manipulation. In the shamanic view, everything is connected—our physical, mental, emotional, and spiritual bodies are all one. In addition, we are one with all of Pachamama. These two different starting points have developed into very different methods of healing and very different realities. How was I going to find a common ground between them?

These issues often came up in my conversations with Shruthi, who was pursuing medical school after shamanic training, the reverse of the path I had followed. She had come on one of the Dream Change Coalition trips I led to the Andes and Amazon of Ecuador. We had flown deep into the jungle, east of the Cutucuu mountain range, to visit communities dedicated to dream change and to maintaining traditional Shuar ways. They were interested in taking action to allow the industrialized nations to reassess the dream that is our world, and they did so by asking us to bring people to their community who were interested in their knowledge in order to experience life as they see it.

One day Shruthi and I were sitting in a longhouse with the rest of the group, eating a typical Shuar lunch. We sat on our haunches near Patricia, a half-Shuar, half-mestizo woman, chatting and enjoying a meal of steamed catfish, hearts of palm and yucca, and chicha.

"What's up with Michael? Why does he always look so sad?" Patricia asked, refering to one of our fellow Dream Change travelers.

"He is a doctor," Shruthi replied, "but since he has seen the power of the shamanic path he no longer practices Western medicine."

"I don't understand," Patricia said, puzzled. "Why would he throw that all away instead of finding a way to use what he has learned in a good way? It doesn't make any sense."

"I understand what you are trying to say," I countered, "but he hasn't found the way to do this. This makes him very sad, very lost."

Shruthi was walking a different path. Unlike Michael, she had not given up and become lost after finding that there are other powerful ways of healing and of viewing health. She was choosing to build upon both her new and old knowledge, but I wondered about the challenges she was facing.

"How are you doing with medical school?" I asked her.

"Some parts have been really weird," she replied. "I don't understand why they put us through some of the lectures. Take medical economics, for example. They told us that we were wasting our lives, that four years would build up to mountains of debt, with less and less chance to make a living, support a family, and have time to be an effective member of a family or community. Why on earth did they tell us all of that after we had already set our intentions and begun the process?"

"I don't know, Shruthi," I answered. "Maybe it's a form of shock teaching, perhaps to weed out the less than dedicated. I remember hearing the same lectures, and I can vouch for those mountains of debt. And the years of call duty every other night certainly did take their toll on my family's and my health, physical and emotional."

"I know it is a huge investment of money, energy, and time," Shruthi said, "and I think I am prepared for that. I still feel that being at Harvard is an opportunity, a door into new possibilities. But the deeper I go in my training, the more uncertain I am becoming about how I can integrate all of what I have learned. I am wondering how I can have a practice that utilizes the shamanic methods of healing that work empirically, but do not fit in the box of the allopathic scientific model."

I told her that I was still seeking the answer to that question myself. Of all fields of medicine, mine—plastic surgery,—was the most obsessed with form and with the human body, most obsessed with dream versus fantasy. Every day as I entered the operating room to perform breast enlargements, lipo-sculpture, and facelifts, I wondered whether I was maintaining my integrity in a culture confined to thinking of change in physical terms. As I spoke to people about what they wanted, why they were considering plastic surgery, I wondered why I had been given this opportunity to grant people their physical dreams, as though I were a genie in a bottle. My perspective of my patients' dreams and their possibilities had expanded, yet it was a struggle to find ways to communicate this in a way that honored their realities and their dreams. I painfully experienced the ways in which the Cartesian illusion of the separation of mind, body, and spirit has led to the separation of the doctor-healer from the patient, a human being with passions, dreams, and spirit.

I struggled to find ways to reconcile these differences. Predictably, my struggle manifested in all aspects of my life. I was a divorced mother of four, with mountains of debt, both personal and professional. I was falling further behind financially each time I took time off from my medical practice to do workshops or to take people to shamanic communities. My practice suffered from my frequent trips abroad, as did my family. It was a time when it was important for my children to feel secure and loved, having been jettisoned from their comfortable life in a home with both mother and father to a life where they shuttled between their mom's and dad's homes with suitcases. As we struggled with my absences, we confronted subjects of security, love, and autonomy that we might never have spoken of otherwise. The struggle created both opportunity and pain.

I remembered that the Mayan elder, shaman Mercedes Barrios Longfellow, had spoken of the challenge faced by the modern healer—to bridge the worlds, to stand and survive in both dreams, to find ways to live with integrity. I was struggling to find the way to proceed with integrity.

Taking Control by Letting Go

Shamanic training is a perpetually ongoing process. Because there is no end to training, only many beginnings, it is difficult to take the leap and call oneself a shaman, especially in our culture, where we are accustomed to degrees and certificates. I, like many other healers, struggled with this. I knew that to identify myself as a shaman would be to embrace authentic power, yet I was also aware that it would leave me very vulnerable—to failure, to ridicule, to accusations of egotistical motivations. This is a huge barrier for all healers, and it is even bigger for those of us in the "North." Our industrialized Western culture tends to be highly individualistic, and the ego is equated with the self. For a shamanic healer, overcoming ego to experience ecstatic states of oneness engenders great power and effectiveness. This essence of shamanism—that of oneness, of overcoming ego—is often what causes us the most fear. What happens if we lose control? What happens if we let go of our ego? Will we go crazy, like my little brother? In our culture this is exactly counter to what we envision as the way to amass power. That made it essential for me to uncover the distinction between authentic and conventional power. I came to realize the necessity of embracing vulnerability in order to find and effectively use power.

My struggle came to a head after my initiation into the circle of Yachaks. When I had pictured my return to the United States after initiation, I had envisioned that I would feel powerful, invincible, and wise. Instead, I found that I had never felt so vulnerable in my life—vulnerable to everyone and everything, to every person, to every situation, to every bill, to every decision. Only when I fell into a firmly patterned persona such as "the doctor" did I find I could function efficiently and without fear. Is that what I had spent all those years training for? What was this all about? I found myself drowning in these and other questions, completely vulnerable in my struggle. I had not expected this at all!

I called John Perkins on the phone one day and broke down, admitting to him that I felt completely vulnerable and powerless, that I must not be on the right track. I felt that feeling the way that I did I couldn't possibly be a healer. I had failed, and it was time to admit that this was not the path for me.

"Perfect!" He astounded me with his spirited response. "Now you're getting somewhere. It's ironic, but this very leap that you'd think would lead to disempowerment, can, when done with intent, result in authentic power. Stay the course. You will find the way."

I was once again thrown off track. I had finally surrendered to the fact that I could never be a shaman, and I was told that now I was finally beginning my training in earnest. Once again, it was the unexpected that brought insight and provided valuable tools, wisdom, and experience. I had overcome many obstacles, passed many classes, learned many lessons that, though tough, were not unanticipated or astounding. They were still inside the box of what I knew of the world. Now I found myself at another interface where nothing made sense. But this time I had learned enough to just let it unfold, to simply be open to expanding my perceptions, my knowledge and skills, and my reality.

Overwhelmed with confusion, I decided to begin all over again. I began to journey in simple ways, little by little, just as I had at the very beginning of my shamanic training. Each night, when I had finished my daily tasks, I would take time to journey. At first, even in this other reality, I felt vulnerable. What answers would I get from my guides? What if they didn't make sense in my day-to-day life? I wondered how I could follow the advice of spirit guides who not only didn't have to live in this realm, but had no stake in the outcome and did not have to face the consequences of their advised action. At times I even fearfully wondered if I was truly going crazy!

Night after night, day after day, I struggled, until I felt as though the barrier crumbled before me. Breakthrough! I came to the realization that in order to have authentic power, I needed to let go—I needed to allow myself to be completely and openly vulnerable! I had been initiated and had died in many senses, yet I was still caught by my old convictions and my old way of viewing the world. I had been operating under the assumption that vulnerability was a bad thing. Now I saw it as a great friend, an ally, a necessity in the birth and growth of authentic power, energy, and wisdom.

Slowly I tried it out. At first I journeyed with small, seemingly inconsequential questions, with little risk to any given outcome, just as if I were journeying for the first time. I proceeded on the advice of my guides in these journeys, and I began to ask more and more consequential questions. I started over, like a novice once again, in this practice of accessing information, power, and energy. Slowly I became more proficient at gathering what I needed at any given time and putting it into action. As I deepened my connection to my guides, they developed in complexity. New guides also presented themselves. As I began to cultivate functional relationships with my guides to effect change, the vulnerability I felt became an important ally in the process of building deep trusting relationships with them. With persistence and integrity, we built mutually confident long-term alliances. It was then that my guides told me that they were manifestations of my inner voice, the voice that had been my friend and helper early in my life, the voice that I had begun to ignore and lose contact with after my little brother went crazy. I had wasted many years and suffered greatly from this period of distrust. Eventually I even came to understand that distrust, like vulnerability, is an important step in all of our lives; but without breaking through it, we never access the authentic power of the universe.

In her book *Meeting the Madwoman,* Linda Schierse Leonard writes of the subconscious "madwoman" within, caged yet seething in uncontrollable anger at her suppression by the consciously righteous "judge." As I slowly accepted my vulnerability, I realized that my fear of letting go—heightened by Benny's insanity—had led me to deeply suppress this archetypal mad part of myself. As I began to embrace her, I came face to face with the archetypal judge that functions to contain her. Over and over, in journeys, in dreams, in my physical life, I encountered both the madwoman and the judge that questions her sanity and validity. What was I to do with her? The answer did not come readily. I struggled daily with the question of what I was to do with all of this experience, knowledge, power, and energy. I knew that a shaman uses it to effect change. How could I effect change in my day-to-day reality? What was my dream?

The answer came to me with great clarity one day in the highest Andes, while I was working with Jose Joaquin Pineda, another birdperson or Yachak shaman. His twinkling eyes shine with deep ancient wisdom wherever he may be, whether walking the paths of Central Park in New York or at his home in the Valley of the Dawn.

I had first met Jose Joaquin, a compadre of John Perkins, a few years earlier on another trip to Ecuador with John. We had been invited to spend the day at the home of Jose and his family. In their long-standing relationship, Jose Joaquin has always accepted John as his equal, his shamanic counterpart in the North. John is godfather to Jose Joaquin's daughter, Soraya, and Jose began training John's daughter, Jessica, when she was only ten years old. I had dysentery once again and was purging heavily from both ends, so we were traveling slowly on our way to his home in Iluman, stopping at every gas station and numerous bushes along the way. I was depleted, nauseated, and in severe abdominal pain.

Like the time when I first came to experience shamanic healing with Alberto Tatzo, my illness afforded me the opportunity to experience a miraculous healing event. We arrived and were greeted warmly as family. The table was set for a festive meal of *cui* (guinea pig, a delicacy in the area), corn, rice, and *chicha de jora* (a sacred fermented corn drink). I explained my situation and was led to a room near the toilet, so that I could continue my purging while they exchanged news.

Eventually I was ready, and Jose Joaquin led me to his healing room. As a Yachak master shaman, he uses methods very similar to those of don Esteban and Maria Juana, yet each of these great shamans has a uniqueness of energy, spirit, and style. A handsome man, Jose Joaquin has a power, wisdom, and compassion that create in him an expansiveness of aura that speaks volumes. This is useful, because he is a quiet man and does not waste words. When he speaks, it is always important, and always a gift. It has been said that you can tell a lot about a shaman by his mesa, or altar table. Jose Joaquin's was set up beautifully, with surgical precision. Bottles of floral essences were carefully arranged, along with fresh flowers, aromatic plants, tobacco, huacas, chonta wood from the Amazon, and feathers. Unlike many of the shamans in the area, Jose makes his own floral essences from his extensive healing gardens, infusing them with love and spirit. His spirit held a gentle yet powerful ancient wisdom. I knew immediately that I was in good hands.

Camaying me with floral water, he began healing me using the elements, feather fans to move *malaire* (bad air), tobacco, huacas, and bells. When I walked into the room I was tense, bent over with abdominal pain and nausea. As he worked, I relaxed into a deep, healing, meditative trance. Soon I found myself asking for something to drink. I was starving!

"How about a beer?" his wife Rosario asked.

"Wonderful," I answered. "Shungo." We celebrated for hours.

Once again I had experienced a miraculous healing, and once again I was in awe. That was my first meeting with Jose Joaquin Pineda.

The day my question about vulnerability and power was answered, Jose Joaquin and I were in the snowcapped mountains, hiking up a winding mountain path at over 11,000 feet. Even though we were near the equator, it was snowing. The air was thin, and I found myself stopping to catch my breath frequently before continuing my struggle to keep up with this elder who chanted and sang while I huffed and puffed. Finally we stopped. Looking out over the mist-covered cloud forests, we felt Pachamama in all her glory, and we rested a moment before beginning our ceremony.

Bundled in a woolen hat, scarf, and gloves, I still shivered. Feeling the familiar vulnerability creep in, I journeyed to my guides. Manuel, an Andean spirit guide who often comes to me playing his flute, arrived immediately. I was physically in his favorite terrain, and he laughed to see me shivering in the snow on the mountain.

"I am so very glad you have come to my home with don Jose," Manuel began, "and that you finally asked me the question that has been troubling you for so long. You really are stubborn, aren't you? Sometimes you like to plod along all by yourself. I was wondering when you'd come for help."

He led me to sit on a large stone. Jose Joaquin began blowing a sacred flute next to me, and in journeytime Manuel joined him. We all rested, both in this reality and in an alternate reality. Breathing in the mountain air and taking in the snowcapped peaks, I slowly was filled with energy and power. Manuel was preparing me for the answer to my question. I readied myself for the transmission of wisdom.

Finally he began to answer: "The key is learning to manifest two opposing ways of being simultaneously—letting go of control while manipulating to effect change; keeping clarity of your dream while allowing the flow of life to guide you; maintaining a strong individual ego while understanding the interconnectedness and oneness of all; surfing the energetic currents of chance and change while driving your collective and individual energy with intent; finding the balance between destiny and the grand forces of nature and what you make of it—your free will." I glanced over at Jose Joaquin and saw from his expression that he agreed. "Listen to your guides," he said to me, "they will help you."

Transforming Our View of Healing

As I was seeking a personal answer to my questions about healing and the path to integration, I was aware of the exponential growth of new information and attitudes in the field of medicine. A reorganization was occurring in the medical community; it was transforming from the standpoint of doctors and of patients alike. In this time of institutional shapeshift, I watched the growing anger of physicians toward the direction of their profession—managed care, medicine as business, more paperwork, and more litigation. Physicians were struggling with higher medical school bills and the rising costs of running a practice. Increasing requirements for staff and equipment paired with decreasing reimbursements meant decreasing earnings. Many doctors were as upset as their patients with the restricted time allotted per patient visit and for interaction with patients. More laboratory studies to review in less time brought more chances for error, more stress, and more fear of litigation. Doctors were feeling anger over turf wars—too many providers offering their wares of expertise in a limited market—and the growing "alternative medicine" community was creating a new turf in the competition among health care providers.

Interest in shamanic and other forms of spiritual and energy healings was growing throughout the world. Indigenous healers, long hidden due to persecution, were coming forward to help and teach. "Alternative" or "complementary" healing techniques were becoming almost mainstream in the United States, with millions of people choosing to go to healers who do energy work, usually paying out of pocket, though increasing numbers of insurance companies were beginning to cover alternative forms of healing.

At the same time I watched the rising anger of patients toward the direction of health care. They were finding it a struggle to get care at all, facing increasing out-of-pocket costs, decreasing coverage, and refused claims, even as monthly insurance costs increased. The growing sense of anger, isolation, and helplessness on the part of both physician and patient was added to the cultural clashes, resulting in miscommunications. The separation between them was widening, and the tone of the doctor-patient contract was becoming more adversarial. I saw that in some cases patients not only were suspicious of the doctor's motives and sincerity, but also were becoming angry, acting as if it were the doctor himself or herself who was creating the disease.

I was struck by the contrast to the shamanic way. After my first shamanic experience with don Alberto Tatzo, I had experienced, witnessed, and performed thousands of shamanic healings. In each and every one I saw benefit to the patient undergoing the healing, sometimes in the manner they had envisioned, sometimes taking another and even more beneficial direction.

I am not implying that patients never become upset with shamans when a healing "doesn't work." They can and do on occasion, especially when faith is lacking. But the diagnostic and healing process is approached from a radically different angle. Shamans work as intermediaries. As the disease is described in spiritual terms, it has more to do with factors on a spiritual plane than anything that the patient did or didn't do. A no-blame system goes a long way toward enhanced communication. Because the healing is done on a spiritual plane, the focus is not on the healer. Although physical prescriptions and actions may be added, the effectiveness of the healing has more to do with the faith of the one being healed than on whether the patient follows the shaman's prescriptions to the letter. A shaman will almost never perform a healing or suggest measures unless asked. There are no frequent clinic visits to check on progress and compliance. In this way, only those ready to be active participants will undergo healings—only those choosing healing, those ready to hear the answers within.

Vision Quest—Redirecting Our Collective Dream

The shamanic model thinks of diseases as messages—individual and communal messages. The diseases of the individual are personal messages coming through the physical form and function of Earth's human inhabitants. The diseases of the planet, such as global warming, El Niño, pollution, and erosion, are communal messages coming through the changing earth herself. What is the message from these diseases? What do we need to hear personally and globally?

I was pondering these questions one day while driving through the streets of Guayaquil with Juan Gabriel.

"Juanito, look at all the people on the streets of the city. Very different from the Amazon, isn't it?"

"Yes, " he said. "So many people hurrying to somewhere, no one smiling, no one stopping to talk."

"It's sad." I added, "I remember growing up in Nairobi. It was such a happy town where everyone smiled. I visited a few years ago, and now it's a sea of human ambition with little opportunity. Children are born on the streets and die on the streets."

"I guess this is the fate of the cities worldwide," he continued. "More people, more poverty, less meaning. There are so many signs of the degradation of communal health, so many children searching for meaning and connection through drugs and gangs. That is why the work of the World Dream Institute is so important. Tell me how that is going."*

"The program is already a huge success in many schools. Our goal is not to tell the children what to dream, but to allow them full expression to clarify their dreams and to learn about the world around them—to connect to the world that is theirs in a responsible and loving way—according to their own personal and communal aspirations. The teachers, principals, and parents are finding that when this forum exists, the children become participants in their schooling. Their process of learning becomes discovery rather than memorization. Test scores improve, behavioral problems ease, and the class becomes a cohesive group setting out to align the learning with their dreams. It has been amazingly successful, even with adolescents— the young men and women who are floundering in questions of where to apply their energy. The World Dream Institute forums give them a chance to explore their possibilities and hone their dreams with a kind of support that has been lost in our culture."

"Yes, I can see the need for that," Juan responded. "My daughters are young, but I hope that they'll get all the support possible to explore their dreams. You know, among the Shuar and even the Quechua, the opportunities for education are so much more limited than they are for our children, and yet their dreams are discussed and explored much more. They are offered beautiful ceremonies to mark their coming of age, and they are supported by the entire community. It sounds like World Dream Institute is

*World Dream Institute (worlddreaminstitute.org) is an offshoot of Dream Change Coalition that works with schoolchildren to provide a forum in which they can explore their dreams and aspirations.

becoming that kind of support to young people in the United States."

We concluded that whatever the method for marking coming of age, whatever the method of vision quest, when the shapeshift in these young people's lives is empowered and they are aided in taking control of their dreams in a good way, with responsibility, then the possibilities for humanity are limitless.

Juan said, "That is so important to help counteract Western culture's determination to control and dominate."

"Yes," I replied, "even in medicine we approach disease with the view of controlling and dominating. We have so many ways to exert control—bactericidals, fungicidals, hormonal manipulation, antibiotics, antipsychotics, surgery. But do we ever really control? In the past century we have controlled the physical events in our bodies through the advances in the field of medicine, improving infant mortality rates and longevity. Now the global population growth is outstripping the earth's capacity to sustain its nonhuman and human inhabitants. Haven't we paid a price for that in terms of our society as a whole? In terms of humanity as a whole? In terms of the planet and all our relations? Have we merely translated physical disease into social disease? Where is the antibiotic for loss of hope? For starvation? For crime and hatred? For loneliness? Infant mortality and average life span were used as indices to assess health in our communities, but what of happiness? What are the indices of happiness?"

We talked of how the United States was founded on principles that included the basic right of the pursuit of happiness, but happiness had become elusive. When did the dream of our ancestors go astray? What happened to the essence of our dream for our communities? Can we change our dream and recapture that essence?

Through the years I found myself coming back to these questions over and over. Slowly the answers emerged from my own life experiences as I learned to see with new eyes and to dream new dreams. I felt the need for Western culture to consciously redirect its dream to a way of health that is truly fulfilling and meaningful. But I was unsure just what that would mean. What would it look like? Feel like? Be?

I remember a heartfelt question posed by a woman in a crowded lecture hall. Ten shamans from South America, John Perkins, and I were giving a lecture at the University of Michigan Medical School for Dream Change Coalition. The talk about shamanic healing practices was coming to an end, and questions were being taken from the audience. A woman stood up and asked if shamanic healings ever failed. I sensed that she wasn't interested in a yes or no answer. What she was interested in was the concept of guilt. She said that her mother had just died a painful death, and by her questions it was clear that her mother had been sad and angry. She asked, "If you believe that you have control over your body, over your life and death, if you believe that the world is as you dream it, won't you feel great guilt when you become ill, or when you die, or—as the healer—when a healing isn't successful?"

My spiritual blood brother, Ipupiara, a great shaman from the Brazilian Amazon basin, took the microphone. He has seen cross-cultural collisions all his life. His father was Portuguese and his mother was indigenous. In his youth he left his village to obtain an education. Returning home with a Ph.D. in anthropology, he also brought with him a tremendous understanding of the world outside his home, of both its wonders and its failings. He then embarked upon shamanic training in his village. After many years of training as a shaman, his path led him back to the industrialized world to fulfill his mission as an ambassador of dream change. He now lives in Washington, D.C., with his wife, Cleicha, a Quechua shaman from the highlands of Peru. There he performs "miraculous" shamanic healings on the throngs of patients who seek him out. He also teaches workshops worldwide, along with working as a consultant for the Smithsonian. If anyone could answer her question, he could.

Ipupiara started to talk of the Bible and of shapeshifting. He spoke about the wonderful shapeshifts in the Bible, and those that we all go through in our lives. He spoke of the final shapeshift in this life—death. He spoke of the beauty and honor of death. "The Amazonian peoples believe that it is far better to die with passion than to live without it. They look forward to their shapeshifts, moving into new beings with each life. In Shuar Amazonian tradition, a well-loved shapeshift is thought to be when an individual dies and becomes the rain. There is no concept of guilt. There is no feeling of the superiority of the human race or of any entity above another, no doubt about our oneness or about our eternal nature as spiritual beings, no disappointment with our shapeshifts at any particular time, our 'lot in life,' our death or impending death. All is sacred, all is honored. We peoples of the Amazon live deeply connected, fully present in the fabric of time. We flow through our lives and deaths with grace, not wasting a single moment. Living in ecstasy at all times. Not bliss, not always joyful, but always ecstatic, always at one with the universe."

The audience pondered this concept. Living and dying in ecstasy, without guilt, sure of our eternal being, knowing our oneness—how different our thoughts of healing and health would be.

7

Remembered Wellness—
Dreaming a New Vision of Health

WHEN I WAS IN MEDICAL SCHOOL, I was often puzzled by the
way we tested the efficacy of any therapeutic method. There was one method
that had an efficacy of which we were always sure. In fact, we were so sure
of its effectiveness that every study included a control for it, to make sure
that the results we were observing were from the method under study. What
is this "sure thing"?

The placebo effect.

What puzzled me is this: If the most effective method of healing is placebo, why aren't we studying it? What exactly is it? Is it one effect or a
combination of several? How can we enhance it? How can we harness it,
direct it, use it?

This phenomenon is finally getting the attention, credit, and study it
deserves. Dr. Herbert Benson of Harvard Medical School writes of his
investigations of the placebo effect in his book *Timeless Healing: The Power
and Biology of Belief.* He writes, "I began to question my assumptions and
the medical community's assumptions. I learned that the placebo effect
worked much better than we usually appreciate. . . ." He calls the placebo
effect "remembered wellness." Remembered wellness! Could it be that one
of the most important steps to being healthy is to understand that we are

programmed for health? And, once having understood and believed it, to consciously desire health?

The other thing that puzzled me was that in four years of medical school and seven years of residency, we never formally discussed health! We never discussed healing! We discussed diseases, a multitude of diseases, but never health.

We did learn about our bodies, anatomically and biochemically. We learned about the miracles of homeostatic balance, of immunology, of neurological and hormonal transmitters, of regenerative growth, of scar tissue formation, of new collagen deposition. We learned about many methods of healing. Yet we never discussed the concept of health or what it is to be healthy.

Wisdom from the Plant Kingdom

While taking elderly patients' histories during medical school and residency, I was astounded by their prescription regimens. A person had to be a genius to figure out how to create a timetable for taking all the medications, and obsessive enough to remember to take them all. As I tried to obtain the history of the prescriptions, the patient would tell of taking one medication for a symptom, then taking another to counteract a side effect from the first medication, yet another to counter the long-term effects of the second medication, and still another for the side effects of the third. It made me wonder whether it was ever going to stop.

Hippocrates—the father of modern allopathic medicine and source of the Hippocratic oath taken by all doctors upon graduation—taught that if you cannot heal your patient with food, then you cannot heal your patient. His "hospitals" are said to have been more like spas, where lifestyle changes were taught and encouraged. The path taken by the medical profession has traveled far from its beginnings. We all know about "comfort foods"—the foods of our childhoods. From an early age I was passionate about food, and culinary creativity was a great artistic outlet for me. My second husband McDonnell taught me about the energy of food. When I cooked, the ingredients and technique may have been exactly the same each time, but he swore he could tell when the food was made with love, and when it wasn't. He was always correct. My passion for food was contagious. When we were first married, McDonnell ate simply and cooked rarely. By the time of our divorce, he was an accomplished chef, having studied under the great chefs of Britain, far surpassing me in skill and knowledge. Yet the biggest lesson he taught me about food was that it is more than its ingredients, more than its chemical composition.

Has modern medicine become blindsided by our single-minded studies of the chemical reaction, the most diminutive perspective, forgetting the whole? When we ingest medications, herbs, and food, is there more to our relationship with them than the minute chemical interactions? As herbalism and natural remedies rise in popularity, many people simply plug herbal combinations into the equation of the modern pill-popping philosophy. The sale of popular herbal remedies such as St. John's wort, echinacea, goldenseal, and ginseng has become a big business, and the earth suffers for it. As a result of this folly, plants are disappearing; some, like goldenseal, are now on the endangered species list.

Is there another way? When we use plants as herbal treatments or as "health food," are we still looking for the best drug, a certain chemical makeup, or is there more to the treatment than a chemical reaction? Is there love and energy in the plants, in the food?

Elva Tatzo, the wife of shaman Alberto Tatzo, is a powerful shaman herself. A great beauty, she exudes a gentle feminine power. In her case, her powerful healing is done mostly in the kitchen. She tells of the days when she was trained as a shaman. Her elders saw in her a unique skill, a connection with and understanding of the healing power of foods. Long sought out by elder shamans for their own personal healing, she now teaches healing through cooking and food combinations to students from around the world.

The renowned herbalist Rosemary Gladstar teaches that our relationship to the foods we eat and the herbs we take is more than a chemical interaction. There is also a spiritual interaction—a connection between the spirit of the plant and our own spirit. Shamans frequently use plants in the course of a healing ceremony, sometimes touching the patient with them and sometimes not. The plants used vary according to the person being healed and according to availability.

Bunches of herbs or bushes are often brushed along the patient's body, cleansing the aura by absorbing "bad" or badly aligned energy. This brushing action is at times forceful, creating a rhythmic beat that can be heard and felt, assisting in trance induction. Connection with the plant spirit world occurs as an important part of the healing process, the ecstatic state of oneness. In the regions around Otavalo, stinging nettles are often chosen for this purpose, adding a strong burning sensation and the development of hives or welts to the process. Shamans also frequently prescribe the use of herbs and other plants for baths and poultices.

In the healing methods of flogging, baths, and poultices, the plant's chemicals certainly interact with the skin and may be absorbed to some extent, yet when herbs are used for brushing they often don't even touch the skin. In those cases, a chemical explanation for the plant's effectiveness is not possible. And there are even times when a plant does not need to be present physically to be useful in healing; instead of touching or ingesting the plant, a connection is simply made by meditating on it or journeying to it.

How does a shaman choose a particular plant and determine the method for its use? If one plant is not available, how is another selected? Shamans' knowledge of the healing powers of plants is certainly not derived from generations of trial-and-error experimentation. There are more species of plants in the Amazon rain forest than anywhere else in the world. With such biological diversity, it is extremely unlikely, statistically speaking, that the plant combinations and preparations ritually used to such great effect would have been found through chance. In addition, although a particular shaman often has a close relationship with certain plant spirits who help him in widely varied cases, there is nothing rigid or fixed about healing regimens. I have often witnessed occasions when the planned herb was not available and the healing was done successfully with others.

When shamans from South America travel to the United States to perform healings, they leave behind the plants with which they are familiar. One time a visiting Otavalan shaman performed a healing at my home and wanted to be able to add herbal remedies to his prescriptions for the patient afterward. The Otavalan market where he would ordinarily send his patients to obtain plants for healing is a very long way from Baltimore. He took a long walk on my property. Coming back to the house armed with bundles of "weeds," he announced that he had learned specific uses and ways to prepare the plants. Not having his familiar helper plants available, alternates were found. Although he had never tried them before, and without any knowledge of herbal uses of temperate plant species, he used these plants with excellent results.

"How did you find out what these plants could do?" I queried this great shaman.

"I asked. I asked the spirit of the plants," he explained.

In the way of the shaman, prescriptions for manipulation in this reality and guidance in actions to further effect change are obtained through journeying. The shaman communes with the plant spirits and receives their help in finding specific uses and techniques appropriate to the individual, the geographic area, and the time.

I asked the Otavalan shaman, "After all the atrocities that we humans as a species have committed against the plant world, why are they so eager and willing to help?"

"It is because in truth we are all one," he answered gently, "and in order to heal, we must all heal—all our relations, human, plant, animal, mineral, the rivers, the air, Pachamama."

Wisdom from the plant kingdom, indeed.

Sound crazy? Perhaps, but it is not really so different from the act of prayer. Every culture has its own way of communing with the spiritual world and its own way of viewing spirit. We are accustomed to the concept of prayer as a way to communicate spiritually, and this seems perfectly normal to us. In different cultures, people communicate in many other ways. When confronted with these cultural differences, can we explain the action of these techniques through our scientific model?

Spirit Medicine

Candace Pert writes about "molecules of emotion" in her book of the same name. A renowned biochemist, she has spent a lifetime searching out receptors for the medications we ingest, and then finding the endogenous or natural form of the medication. She has found that in order for any drug to have an effect in our body, our body has to have a receptor for it. Moreover, if there is a receptor, then our bodies must naturally make a chemical that fits even better into that receptor than the ingested one, with even more potent effect. Endorphins are a good example. It was learned that our bodies have an opiate receptor into which drugs like heroin fit. Then endorphins—created by the body itself—were found. Always present in varying amounts and capable of creating a natural "high," endorphins are far more potent and effective than even heroin. Through the mind-body connection, our body's chemical composition is shapeshifted, internally modulated moment by moment, through our nervous system and blood system, through hormones and immune cells, through virtually every cell and organ system in our bodies, all of which are impacted by our emotions and thoughts.

Is this the scientific model that explains the placebo effect studied by Herbert Benson? Does it provide the key to understanding how we can shapeshift more effectively, changing our internal chemical composition without ingestion of external chemicals? Is there even more to healing than chemical interactions? Are the changes in our physical bodies accompanied by changes in our mental, emotional, and spiritual bodies? Can we be better facilitators of healing if we address all the changes, all our interactions, all our relations? Is this the method of creative visualization and relaxation techniques? How can we drive this energy more consciously and enhance our innate healing systems?

I read of a study that was performed on patients with rheumatoid arthritis. The patients were separated into two groups. One group was asked to write in a journal daily as a way to express their thoughts, their concerns, and their feelings. That was the only difference in the treatment of the two groups. Severity of symptoms for patients of both groups was monitored. At the end of the study, it was reported that the group who released through journaling had significant reduction in their symptoms and in their arthritis. How were their own immune systems revved up to fight the inflammation? We might explain this through Candace's "molecules of emotion." In her model, we can direct our healing energy, and we can learn to do it more and more effectively.

It would be hard to use Candace's model, however, to explain the findings related to long-distance prayer. A study was done whereby patients in a coronary care unit were divided into two groups and monitored. One group was prayed for, from a distance and without their knowledge. At the end of the study there was a significant difference in the outcome between the two groups, scientifically documenting the beneficial power of prayer. What could not be explained scientifically, however, is the mechanism of that benefit. It can't be the placebo effect, because the patients didn't know that they were being prayed for. This benefit can only be a spiritual manipulation, healing the spiritual body on the spiritual plane—the same manipulation that shamans use in their healings.

Directing Energy with Intent

What do we do with this information? What are we doing when we try to heal another or ourselves? What is health? What is it to be healthy? What is it to be healed? Eventually every doctor is confronted with this question—what the heck are we doing, anyway? Is the model of engaging in a war against disease, where we lose some battles and win others, really adequate to describe the process of healing?

How could this be? Our bodies are healing machines! We are physically bombarded moment by moment by "outside" organisms, by micro and macro trauma, by ultraviolet and other forms of radiation. Daily we meet with a multitude of insults to our physical integrity. We live in concert with huge colonies of bacteria, yeasts, and other living beings, and we swap molecules with those "outside" of us every second. The cells and molecules making up our skin, the outer organ, are completely different from those that made it up a year ago. We eat. The plants and animals that were once separate from us become a part of us; they are distributed and changed as needed, with some stored for later use.

We grow older, fatter, thinner, more muscular, less muscular. We repair our blueprints by continually fixing the breaks in our DNA and RNA. We become ill; we get better. We grow tumors; we shrink tumors. Changes in physical balance and healing continuously occur in miraculous ways—continual shapeshifts. We can now explain so much, yet many things still do not fit into our model of the body. I began to see that the answers might lie in dropping for a moment the need to explain, and in accepting new models of the world around us and within us. We needed to make a quantum leap experientially and explore new definitions of health and new tools for healing.

Can we become more conscious of how we direct these miraculous healing processes, how we shapeshift? Can we add conscious intent? Increasingly the Western scientific community is studying these questions and others. Lamas and yogis have long been studied for their ability to consciously direct their "involuntary" bodily processes, such as raising their body temperature high enough to melt snow or decreasing their body temperature to radically slow metabolic rates. I have seen shamans change their physicality, turning into snakes, jaguars, and bats. Can we also do these things?

In actuality we do these things every day; we simply need to practice putting our hands on the steering wheel and directing our energy with intent. Einstein taught us that everything is energy and we are all one. We can make pragmatic use of this knowledge.

Today many forms of healing are available, including methods that work empirically but are difficult or impossible to explain in terms of the allopathic view of the body's workings. Methods such as chiropractic, acupuncture, reflexology, Reiki, and even shamanic healings are increasingly asked for by the public and are even being used in hospitals across the country.

"Miraculous" healings are now seen so frequently that they are no longer miraculous. I have seen people use shamanic methods to shrink tumors, resolve chronic back pain, cure fibromyalgia and other debilitating chronic diseases, help patients lose weight, look younger, regain hearing from deafness, and drop addictions . . . the list is endless. What are these shapeshifts? Are they simply redirecting energy flow, removing blockages so that our own innate "miraculous" healing powers can flow? What does the healer actually do to take away disease nearly instantaneously?

Any shaman will tell you that they themselves are doing nothing! They take no personal credit for the healings. They are paid for their time and effort, for they put themselves at grave risk, often taking on imbalances in their own energy field through their work, even causing themselves and their families personal or social disease. Yet they will always tell you that they are only facilitating the healing—the credit goes to Pachamama (Mother Earth/universe/time), to the Great Spirit, to the forces of nature, or to God—and to the patient him- or herself.

Crossing the Threshold of Change

Through years in medical practice, I had come to realize that by the time my patients pick up the phone to make an appointment with me as a plastic surgeon—or to call any healer, for that matter—two very important steps have occurred first. First, they have decided that something is awry in their life, something is not as they want it to be; and second, they have decided to do something about it. They want change and they are asking for it. They are at a gateway, a magical place. Only they hold the key to the gate. But we as healers should understand this as an opportunity to help them ease the key into the door and to assist their passage through the gateway. I began to fully appreciate what a beautiful and rich opportunity this magical time of transformation is for both patient and healer—an opportunity to change with conscious intent and to be conscious of our true dreams.

After creating an external change with cosmetic surgery, I have often watched my patients change internally in many ways. I have seen them develop new stances, new ways of holding their bodies, new ways of walking and talking, new ways of relating to the world. New relationships, new jobs, new passions—they were moving into and realizing their dreams.

Of course there are also patients who don't go through the gateway to a new way of being. They come in asking for an external change, but after the surgery changes the way they look, they are disappointed to find that their life doesn't change. They don't change.

I have found that the wish for life change is usually subconscious in our culture. At their first interview with me, most people speak very literally about changing their bodies surgically, detaching the physical change from any effect on their inner selves—on their emotional, mental, or spiritual bodies. But this detachment is an illusion—we cannot separate our physical bodies from our thoughts, our emotions, or our spirituality.

The plastic surgery patients who do not walk through the gate continue to be unhappy. What happens when their lives do not change in the manner in which they desired, consciously or subconsciously? They come back for more surgery or seek other doctors or other disciplines of healing. For a while I thought this plight was specific to plastic surgery, but as time went on I found that it is common in all healing traditions. Whether it is internal medicine, psychotherapy, chiropractic, acupuncture, Reiki, shamanism, or any other kind of healing, some patients gracefully flow into change while others defy change with a resistance so strong that nothing can move them.

And yet they had come asking for change. They wanted change. But they didn't want to change themselves. The old adage "You can't have change without change" is true. If you want to find the way to change your life, you have to change your ways.

If we take the position that there is a connection between our spirituality and our physicality, what is the meaning of disease?

I have seen numerous cases, in both allopathic and "alternative" medicine, of "cures" being followed by a relapse of the same disease or the development of another disease—cancers being cured only to be followed by a different cancer; a shapeshift into a younger, thinner, more beautiful body followed by aging or weight gain; chronic pain relief followed by another chronic disease.

These experiences seem to indicate that without addressing the whole person, permanent "cures" cannot succeed. Could it be that there isn't, as we have long assumed, a separation between our physical, emotional, mental, and spiritual bodies? Could it be that we can adjust the alignment between these bodies, remove blockages, and enhance energy flow? Could it be that in order to effect a long-term shapeshift patients need not only to ask for healing and to clarify what healing means for them, but also to truly want it?

Listening to Spiritual Messages

If each of us is a miraculous healing machine, might a lack of balance, a disease, really be a gift? A message? It may be an opportunity to redirect our lives and our dreams or an opportunity simply to take a rest. I began to see that we need to listen to these messages. If we simply remove a disease with treatment but don't listen to the inherent message, another message may be presented to us, one that is perhaps more severe and more difficult to ignore. When a deformity cannot be repaired, the disease cannot be cured, or when we die—can the disease itself hold a purpose? Can even death be a healing?

One of my workshop participants, Fran, distinctly heard her name being called while journeying. "It was too freaky!" she complained. "But Fran," I responded, "I have heard you ask for a sign from God many times, for a message. This may be the message you have been asking for, and it has reached you clearly and audibly. If this is your response, how long do you think you'll have to wait to get another?"

In shamanic communities, most messages are considered to come in forms far more subtle than spoken voices. As we begin to ask and listen, we can "hear" more and more personal, communal, and global messages. Messages come to us through life's synchronicities, through climate change, even through disease. How many people have had a heart attack only to say that it was a "wake-up call" for them, that they were able to see their lives and their choices more clearly after that? When I hear people saying that they are now able to live life more fully, not taking their lives and relationships for granted any more, I wonder if there might have been more subtle messages, more subtle "wake-up calls," in the years preceding the heart attack, that—if they had been heard—would have resulted in the person's turning sooner to a truly healthy life, a life lived more fully, a life lived with more conscious dreams and choices.

In shamanic cultures, the question "why" is always asked when someone becomes ill, or when there is an accident, a change in the climate, or social unrest. I recall the story of an American woman walking in a marketplace in Bali who fell, twisting her ankle. A passerby stopped to help her. "Why did you fall?" he asked. The woman replied, "I don't know, perhaps I missed my footing." The man took her to a nearby healer. As the healer prepared a paste to rub on her swelling ankle, he asked her, "Why did you fall?" "Well, I don't really know," she said. "Perhaps it was these new shoes; I am not used to them." The next day the swelling was a little better, but not completely. When the taxi driver taking her to visit a nearby village noticed her ankle, she told him that she had fallen in the marketplace. "Why did you fall?" he asked. "I don't know. Perhaps the rocks were laid unevenly on the path, perhaps it was the jostling of the crowd . . . why is everyone asking me why I fell?" she questioned, a little puzzled and annoyed.

"It is the most important question," replied the taxi driver. "I can take you to a great healer in my village, but he also will ask you why you fell. Until you are able to hear the message, you will be unable to heal completely. Perhaps your ankle will eventually get better, but another message will come in one form or another."

In our culture we seem to have many answers. When asked why we had an accident or a disease, or in the face of global climate change, we give many answers—faulty tools, faulty user, genetics, biochemical and anatomic mishaps, pollution, the shrinking ozone layer. Yet these are answers to the question *how*, not *why*. *Why* questions lead to a message. What is the message? What is spirit telling us through the language of our physical existence? How can we connect more fully to our physical existence and begin to hear God?

The answers are within ourselves. We need only to ask, open up to the answers, and pay attention.

The Sacred Union of the Divine Mother and the Divine Father

My personal struggle for answers continued, and I could not hear, or would not listen to, the answers of my own guides. I searched elsewhere for answers. My search took me all over the world, asking many "experts," but still I could not hear, still I would not listen. The answers seemed too easy to be valid. Then I had an intense vision that clarified my mission and my position as a healer. A serpent came to me to impart knowledge of the evolution of humanity's communal dreams and of our future direction.

The serpent arose from the earth and spoke to me: "In the last few millennia humankind has reached upward to heaven as a separate place, striving to connect with spirit in the form of the divine father, the creator, the authority. Always directing energy upward, humanity developed a hierarchical notion of the energetic centers of the body, the chakras."

I felt like I was a student again in a lecture hall. I had never had a vision that was so full of information before, so intellectual.

"In reaching upward, human beings strove to strengthen the upper three chakras—those representing the will, the mind, and cosmic connection with spirit. At the same time they spiritually pulled away from the lower three chakras—those representing the ego, the physical experiences of sensuality and sexuality, and our relationships—relationships with each other, including all of the earth's inhabitants, as well as with spirit in the form of Pachamama, the divine Earth Mother."

The serpent paused, coiling into a ball for effect. I waited, watching her and feeling pulled downward with her as she coiled into Mother Earth, accepting the mother's nourishment and support. She continued, "Through millennia of pulling away from the lower chakras, humans developed the notion of hierarchy, identifying the upper chakras and the cosmic connection to the divine father as all-important and as endangered by the lower chakra energies. This resulted in a great chasm, a division between the masculine and feminine spirit in every human being. It also resulted in the development of fear—fear of the power of the physical senses, and fear of the lower chakra energies, now long suppressed and boiling. The divine mother has been ignored and maddened by this divisive power play in which the connection to the divine father is deemed more important than the connection to the divine mother; and the human mind and will are given more importance than human physicality, relationship, and sensuality. This war of competing energies meets at the middle, or fourth, chakra, the heart. The heart is the frontline in this battle."

"Hold on a minute," I interrupted her. "You say the heart has been the middle ground for thousands of years? Is that why humans have dedicated so many of our ballads and stories to the age-old love story, the split between man and woman?"

"Is this frontline in the battle of humanity's dream masculine or feminine?" the serpent asked in response. "Is there sex without love? Does sex have anything to do with love? The questions have been sung in ballad after ballad, asked in tale after tale, life after life.

"These questions have no answers, only personal truth. The tides of this truth are changing. It is time now for humanity to connect once more to the divine mother, to open the heart fully, to feel spirit in the physical realm with all the senses, and to strengthen the lower chakras. You have already felt the power of embodying your spirit and thus connecting in every way, physical and nonphysical."

As she spoke, I could feel the power of the sacred waters and volcanoes of my initiation pulse through me. I remembered how on that day in the Valley of the Dawn I felt spirit deeply grounded in my body, in Mother Earth, while at the same time I experienced a cosmic connection to the divine father and the upper chakras.

The serpent concluded, "You have become deeply rooted in energetic strength, like a tree firmly planted in the earth, reaching to the sky. You have felt the connection between all of our relations, human and otherwise. This is life—the sacred union of the divine mother and the divine father, spirit embodied."

Finally it all made sense. I was being asked to be a messenger for indigenous wisdom, for the wisdom of deep connection to the spirit of the earth; my work was to aid in changing our communal dream. Before this vision, I could think of no less likely candidate for that messenger than me—a cosmetic plastic surgeon! After the dream, it all fell into place.

The years of working as a plastic surgeon, listening to people tell me their physical dreams, their quest for change through the physical, had showed me the profound disconnection between the spiritual and the physical in our culture. I had been taught by all the patients through the years who had shapeshifted so very gracefully after the physical change of surgery, allowing this shapeshift to flow through their whole beings, to reverberate through their whole lives, connecting the physical with all aspects of their lives and souls. And I had been taught by the patients who did not shift, who became obsessed with their physicality and overwhelmingly unhappy, as if their wish for a physical shapeshift were a misdirected dream, disconnected from their soul's purpose.

My life in this highly materialistic culture, a culture obsessed with "stuff," with our bodies and our possessions, had made me suspicious of the physical. But shamanism had reintroduced me to the possibility of living in a very different reality, connected to the physical, yet devoid of materialistic obsession. Finally I saw my life as a pathway to this very point in the flow of time. Our obsession with the physical arises from the illusion of separation from spirit. When we live in the box of separation, we dream our aspirations in physical terms. Our dreams narrow in focus until they are completely disconnected from our spirits, from our soul's path.

I had been shown the answer, through my own life and through the message in my vision. Ironically, in order to find true fulfillment in our pursuit of happiness, to eliminate our obsessions with the unsatisfying materialistic part of life, we need to become more physical, not less. The path to enlightenment could no longer be seen only in terms of physical and emotional deprivation or located in a place outside of ourselves and our earthly existence. To embody our spirits, we need to connect more fully and deeply to the physical through our senses at every moment of our lives; we need to awaken to the spiritual nature of this physical experience called life.

East Meets West

It was not long after this that I found myself once again listening to my inner voice despite conventional wisdom. I decided to travel to the Himalayas, this time teaching alongside John Perkins on a trip lovingly orchestrated by Sheena Singh, who had previously participated in our annual Intensive Shapeshifting Course. She had found clarity about this portion of her life's dream during our course and had been inspired to organize a trip for Dream Change to Ladakh, which lies high in the Himalayas. Accompanied by twenty-nine other Dream Change supporters and by Thuptan Lama, a gelong or high lama whom we affectionately called Lamaji, we found ourselves sitting in front of a Tibetan shaman.

The shaman was swaying in deep trance, invoking Dakini deities and making offerings of wine, flour, incense, and rice. She was chanting and praying, sucking against skin with narrow copper tubes. The spiritual extractions she was making were concretizing into physicality, and she spit out black tarlike fluid with hard stones. The tools and methods I was witnessing were virtually the same as those used in South America in the high Andes and deep Amazon, yet these peoples had had no communication with each other, at least none on the physical plane. They had each learned their methods through psychonavigation and meditation, gathering information and power from other realities to create change in this one.

"Do you have a question?" Lamaji translated.

"Yes, I do. I am a doctor who practices Western medicine. And I perform shamanic healings. How can these be integrated? Where do they come together?" I asked.

"They don't," the shaman said simply. "Both are necessary."

I felt as though a heavy weight had been lifted from me. I had been struggling for years to see why I was being led on two seemingly widely disparate paths, and wondering how I could possibly connect the two.

Suddenly I saw. Physical healing through medication or manipulation is not effective without addressing the emotional and mental aspects. Psychological counseling for the emotional and mental bodies is not effective without addressing the physical aspects. Neither of these is effective without addressing the spiritual aspects—without removing blockages and enhancing energy flow.

For the healer, the shamanic access to knowledge, power, and energy enhances all of these processes—physical, emotional, mental, psychological, and spiritual. Perhaps more important, the shaman's access enhances the process of the one being healed, by asking why, hearing the messages, and taking appropriate action. It was my role to live with presence and to aid other human beings to live in grace, flowing along with the fabric of time that is the present. Living my own dream meant sharing the way to fully embody spirit so that our bodies know experientially the true healing of living in ecstatic spiritual connection.

Living in Health

Living and studying with the shamans, traveling and working with other Dream Change Coalition people, and facilitating trips and workshops has opened me to new forms of learning. While I have by no means reached a final destination, and know now that there is no final destination, I have come closer than ever to understanding the meaning of healing, of being healthy. To live in health most effectively, we need to nurture our complete self—our spiritual, emotional, mental, and physical bodies.

We nurture our spiritual body by finding and enhancing connection, experiencing our oneness in nature and in spirit. The method used is not important; the connection is the key. Some find it helpful to pray, some to meditate, some to walk in nature or sit by a body of water. In shamanic communities this communion is continuous and is a part of every moment, of every breath of every experience, of every feeling and thought.

We nurture our emotional body by living from the heart, moment to moment. We have been well trained as thinkers, and we need to use this thinking ability at appropriate times, such as I do when formulating a prescription for medicine or coming up with an operative plan. But to enhance our health, we must let go of that thinking when emotions arise; we must simply feel. Whether the feeling is anger, happiness, or sadness, we are meant to feel each moment fully, then release our feelings. It is the storing and stagnating, the ruminating from the mind instead of the heart, the shoulds and shouldn'ts, the coulds and couldn'ts, that block us from true release. Nurturing our emotional body means living each moment fully and finding safe and compassionate ways to feel, embrace, and then release our emotions. Take time to get out of your mind; let each thought go and come back to your sensations. Feel your emotions and expand your heart, identifying and breaking down walls continually to establish a fully open and unencumbered heart and spirit.

We also need to nurture our mental body. Here is where it gets sticky for us. We in the industrialized nations are very strong—perhaps overdeveloped—in the mental body. Our technological knowledge and ideas are unsurpassed. Yet it is important for us to find balance now in order to find health. Depression and obsessive-compulsive disorders are rampant and increasing in our society due to this imbalance. The key is not in discarding the mental acuity we have gained but in expanding our hearts and our sensual awareness. "Feel, don't think"—this is a mantra you can use whenever you find yourself getting confused or distressed. On the other hand, many spiritual teachers in more heart-based cultures guide their students to think more and feel less to find balance. With balance, we can find mental health.

It is vital in the process of nurturing our mental body to consciously and continually choose our perspective, our eyes, and our thoughts. Our thoughts direct our experiences, thus creating the world that we perceive. Because each person has a unique perspective, the same event will be seen and experienced differently by different people. By consciously

choosing our perspective and our thoughts, we can change what we create—our experiences, our lives, our worlds.

We need to nurture our physical bodies by listening to the signs and
messages coming from our changing bodies and their reactions, taking action
or modifying action as needed. That naturally includes eating well, living
an active and physical lifestyle, and seeking help when necessary to treat
disease or enhance energy flow. It also means having fun, feeling with all our
senses, moment by moment being fully aware of the sensual nature of life.

When our body gives us a message of imbalance, we can realign ourselves through whatever means appeal to us and result in the most positive feedback from our body. Many possibilities exist—chiropractic, body-
work, Reiki, acupuncture, aromatherapy, shamanic healings, allopathic
medicine—the methods that feel right will vary between persons. We can
have fun exploring and take the actions that feel right. Of course, the
action needed for the physical body at times may include chemical or
physical manipulation. Whatever the route, we need to work together
with our health care workers for our own health, remembering that we
must take primary responsibility. As we become more accustomed to listening to the messages from our body, taking action and assessing the
results of the action from ongoing messages, we become much more comfortable in taking primary responsibility for our own healthy being.

Healing as a Way of Being

When I first understood that we can set our intent and align our innate
healing capacities, I started to wonder why we need to go to healers and
especially why shamans themselves can become sick. The answer that came
from my guides has to do with the fact that we are all one. To try to heal all
alone isolates us from our communities, from communing with each other
and with all our relations. As healers we need to understand this deeply and
experientially; through our communion we will find the knowledge, power,
and energy that we need to help each other align our energy, break down
walls and lift barriers, and flow into health. I have found again and again

that people in shamanic communities don't feel guilty about disease or hardship. They experience it and live it. Challenges or stress are a necessary part of life. Without them, we wouldn't get up in the morning; there would be no incentive to do anything. Stress itself is not harmful, but distress, or a feeling of "why me," of disappointment or anger at our circumstances, is very harmful. Remember that illness may be an important message, or you may just be ill, may just need to slow down a little. There is no guilt in being ill; it is just another life experience, with possible lessons and insights to gain.

Why did John Perkins take me to Alberto Tatzo in the Andes to be healed instead of healing me himself; why do I continue to take people to the shaman elders around the world for healing and teachings? The same question could be asked about other initiated healers. The answer is that we have all made commitments to honor our elders and our teachers, the shamans, when we are in their lands or invite them to ours. Although we all practice the healing methods they have taught us, whenever they are available, we make a point of deferring to them. We do this to honor them, and because it helps us to continue learning and feeling our connection with them, with the shamanic path, with the elements, with our guides, and with Pachamama.

Doctor, heal thyself? No. Doctor, heal thy profession, and enable all of our healing, together, all of us. How then can we define healing? In asking this question, I could initially see more clearly what healing isn't. Healing is not perfection, something to strive to attain—a perfect body, perfect health, a perfect marriage, perfect emotions, a perfect life. Healing is more a way of being. Healing is accepting the circumstances of our lives. Healing is releasing—not holding on to pain, anger, frustration, or guilt. It is moving through disease, moving through lessons. Healing is listening to the messages, then moving forward with action. Healing is finding and maintaining balance by embracing all of ourself, all of our energies, and allowing free flow directed by clear intent. Healing is clarifying our dreams and then taking action, leaping fully into them with responsibility.

Healing is experiencing and deepening connection with each other and with all our relations—human, animal, plant, mineral. It is connection with the elements and with spirit, and moving into our oneness, our divinity. We are truly one. Only when each and every child of the universe is healthy can we say that *we* are healthy. This includes not just humans but also the children of the plants and animals, the children of the stones and waters. Only when the earth itself and all her inhabitants are healthy can we say that we are healthy.

An Oath for True Healing

My path has taken me from the Hippocratic oath, sworn by all new physicians, to the proposal of a new oath, to be taken by the healer and the one to be healed alike.

I commit:
To listen to the opportunities given to me through the gift of disease.
To feel the natural magic and miracle of my innate healing capability.
To nurture myself and all my relations: physically, emotionally, mentally, spiritually.
To dream with conscious intent, thereby directing my personal and communal energy.
To open to all realities, with new eyes, expanding consciousness.
To embrace all of myself, directing free flow of opposing energies with clear intent.
To live fully each moment in ecstasy and with the perspective of eternity.
To awaken to and honor our oneness.
To embody spirit in this physical experience called life.

8

Shapeshifting Our Lives

THE FLAME FLICKERING ON THE CIRCULAR ALTAR that we had prepared in the middle of the floor indicated that the helping spirits had arrived. Huacas of stone were spread out on a regal Congolese mat within the circle, which was formed by textile strips. Feathers representing the element air and bowls of wine and water completed our mesa or altar. The heady scent of copal incense filled the room, the familiar acrid aroma of Maya sacred ceremony.

Twenty-six participants lay on the floor journeying in deep trance while my assistant Robert and I drummed a steady beat. We were working on shapeshifting, something that we all do unconsciously every day. In this workshop we were finding ways to shapeshift with conscious intent. I had already explained that we would be journeying shamanically, accessing energy, power, and information for the purpose of effecting change in this reality, that change being our dream or intent. And I had clarified the distinction made in shapeshifting work between fantasy and dream, describing fantasy as a vision that we can enjoy fully in journeys but that would take us to situations we would rather avoid if we gave it energy and manifested it in this physical reality. A dream, on the other hand, is a vision that we feel we truly want to give energy to and manifest.

The beginning steps in learning how to shapeshift are the same no matter what the dream, whether one's dream is to shapeshift into a jaguar, shrink a tumor, drop an addiction, write a book or create any project, embody a personality and persona that we admire, or effect change in our communities and institutions:

1. clarifying and setting intent

2. accessing help in the form of guides and elemental energies

3. listening to messages from our guides, our bodies, our environment, and all our teachers to find out about ourselves and how we manage our energy—where it is unbalanced, blocked in flow, leaking, or misdirected

4. identifying and breaking down barriers or blockages

5. finding and maintaining balance

6. accepting the energy that is us now, our bodies and situations, and coming to know and feel the energy of the shapeshift as if already manifest—being rather than becoming

7. creating a supportive environment for maintaining the energy of that shapeshift

8. embracing the extremes of our many dualities, allowing both sides of each to coexist

9. sharing by expressing the dream—in other realities through prayer or ceremony, and in this reality through conversation or through other means of expression such as painting, music, and dance

10. embodying the dream by committing to do some action every day to further the dream here and now

11. letting go of expectations of form, vision, and timetable

This was our task for the workshop—to learn the individual ways that for each of us work well in performing these steps. I had facilitated many workshops like this one at the Omega Institute, and each time I learned more and more through the process.

Clarifying and Setting Intent

In this first journey, each person began with clarifying and setting their intent, preparing to send the energy of that intent out and then to let it go. Said another way, they were readying for prayer. Then they were looking deeply at the shape that they aspired to be—whether they envisioned it as a physical, emotional, mental, spiritual, or communal shift—by examining what the shapeshift would look like if it were already manifest.

The people sat up, a little dazed but excited from the journey. Each participant appeared to be filled with energy, power, and information to share in circle with the group that was already becoming a close-knit tribe, each bringing to the circle differing insights, experiences, and talents.

I sat down and addressed them, saying, "I want to start by explaining why Robert and I are called facilitators of this workshop, and not teachers. Our teachers are all around us in every thought, every imagination, every feeling, every sensation, every situation, and every experience. Our teachers take many forms—our lovers, our enemies, our children, the person sitting next to you, the stranger in the line at the bank, the person at the front of the classroom or lecture hall, the books and music that we take in, the rivers, the rain, the trees, the animals, the rocks, the weather, our diseases. You may also learn from me, just as I will learn from you. I want to make sure that I thank each and every one of you for what you will teach me through this workshop. Thank you."

With that, they began to share their journeys and express their dreams.

Barbara, an inner-city school principal, voiced her dream as finding inner peace and taking that with her at all times.

Woody, a college professor, spoke of his proposed shapeshift by describing the attributes to which he aspired. "I want to be a vital part of the community. This is my second time at this workshop. Last time my dream was vitality. This time it is community as well."

Mary, a nurse, spoke of her wish to lose and keep off the unwanted weight that had plagued her since the birth of her last child, despite her attempts with every method of weight reduction she could find.

Diana, a musician, wanted to work on looking youthful and pretty, and especially to lessen the bags under her eyes.

David, a businessman, wanted to find his mission in life.

Peggy, a mother and homemaker, wanted to be free of the fear that she continued to feel in many life situations since an accident several years earlier. "It's not that I was fearless before," she explained. "I've always been a timid person, but I have to admit that I've always envied those people who are able to push the envelope. I don't know what happened that day. I'd been in other accidents before that one, one even worse. But for some reason—ever since that day when the car slid down the valley—I have felt like a different person. I'm terrified on the road, but it doesn't stop there. Everything seems to scare me now. I want to change, to be like those whom I envied in my youth. I want to be fearless and to be able to push the limit, to take risks, to live my life full tilt."

Accessing Help

After all the participants had shared their dreams for the shapeshift they wanted to work on during the week, we readied ourselves for another journey. "We are going to learn to access help," I explained. "Help is available to us all, at all times. We simply need to recognize it, to be open to it, and to ask."

Robert described the journey: "This time we are going to do a retrieval journey. Retrievals are an important part of shamanism. There are many kinds, such as a soul retrieval, which can be risky and is much more specialized. Simple retrievals, journeying for someone else, are often easier than journeying for yourself, because you have absolutely no attachment to the outcome!" He went on to explain how to journey in pairs to retrieve a shapeshifting huaca, a spirit guide, for a partner. "Although *huaca* is a Quechua word for a sacred object, often a stone, in spirit it could come in the form of absolutely anything, an animal, an object, a person, a color . . . whatever comes to you, ask it if it is your partner's shapeshifting huaca. If it isn't, ask if it can lead you to your partner's spirit guide, and continue until you get a sense that you have found the right one."

We began to drum for the journey, and one by one the participants sat up and camayed the spirit guide that they had retrieved for their partner.

"Wow, that was as easy as you said it would be." Mary laughed. "It came so quickly, I had it in mind even before I lay down."

"Now share the experience with your partners!" I instructed.

The animated conversation in the room was already shapeshifting the group as they began to relax into the natural ease of journeying and of connecting with spirit guides. After the pairs switched and retrievals were performed for the other partners, we sat again in circle.

"What is a spirit guide, exactly?" Barbara asked. "I immediately recognized what my partner described to me as being an invisible friend that I played with as a kid. I often speak to her still, and I have known her as my angel, although I feel like she is really my inner self."

"The assistance of a spirit guide comes in different forms for different people," I answered. "In my experience it isn't helpful in the process of shapeshifting to debate the intellectual ramifications of the way in which spirit guides appear. They are shapeshifters, too. Over time, they change; they come and go; and you will get other guides. Our culture is so heavily mind based that we are top heavy. In order to balance that in this workshop and this work, we emphasize feeling rather than thinking. The process works. Open your hearts, connect to spirit in the earth, and feel deeply—emotionally, sensually, and spiritually. We can trust that our guides know which forms are most helpful to us at any given time."

"I got a white feather," said Woody, "and I have one right here!"

"I got an owl," said Peggy, "and I collect owls. How could she have retrieved that for me? She doesn't know me! This is fun—validating and empowering to say the least."

"As with any relationship," I said, "you will find that the bond between you and your guides deepens with time. A mutual trust will develop as you ask for help and receive it. Spend time with your guides. Make friends. Have fun—each one has a different personality. And remember to ask questions. It has been my experience that they rarely butt in unasked for, yet they are always present and ready to assist."

"It took me a very long time. I kept wondering why everyone else was getting up when I had barely begun to find the lower world," Dave lamented.

"Do you have a practice of journeying?" Robert asked.

"Yes, I have been doing it for years," he answered.

"If you have a way that works for you, go ahead and use it. Don't fix what ain't broke," Robert answered. "But you also don't have to be rigid in your methods if others present themselves to you over time that are effective for the task at hand. Sometimes you may not have the time to do all the steps that you learned to do. It may not be necessary to distinguish the lower from the upper world."

"This comes up frequently in our Dream Change workshops," I added. "There are many great teachers of shamanism who have effectively taught people nationwide, using somewhat rigid rules and steps. That is fine. But many participants who have learned that way have a hard time with the fact that in our workshops we have no rules. No rules at all. We feel that whatever presents itself to you is the right thing for you. This is the way that we were taught by the Shuar, by the Quechua, and by teachers of many other shamanic communities who are not as stuck in intellectual thoughts as we are. They are certainly not rigid, and they are powerful beyond belief. Try seeing what comes to you. Spirit will guide you well. You can even ask your guides about technique and see what comes up. They are your greatest teachers, and they are there all the time. You are one with them."

Robert added, "Just as we are one with our guides, we are also one with the basic elements—earth, air, fire, and water. These energy flows are universal in shamanic culture and are very helpful in effecting change. In the next journey we will begin to access these elemental energies, which are always available for use in healings and other shapeshifts.

"Let the elements cleanse you—let it all go! Feel the release of all tensions, all stresses, all worries that have built up in you from the day you were born. You don't need them! They are blocking your energy from flowing to your dream."

They journeyed to the elements fire, air, water, and earth, feeling the release of unwanted energies and tensions. Refreshed, they sat ready for the next journey.

"Remember the effect of this journey whenever you feel blocked," I suggested. "You may have released all unwanted emotions and energies, but new ones may come at any time. You can use this same technique at home, at work—whenever and wherever you need it. It can be done effectively in seconds if needed. I use it often. All of the techniques that you are learning this week are useful in everyday living, and I encourage you to find where and when they fit into your own lives, for the rest of your lives."

Flowing with the River of Love

"As you work with elemental energies over time, you will notice the energy that arises as they all come together. This is the fifth element, known as *ushai* in Quechua, space in the Bon tradition, and Arutam by the Shuar. It is the feeling of oneness, of nirvana. This universal oneness is powerful. You could call it the elemental love energy.

"We will access this river of love right now in a journey. Recall what it feels like to be head over heels in love. You might remember a time of romantic love or the feeling of love for a parent, a child, or a puppy . . . remember a time when love flowed strongly through you. Begin your journey there, and then feel the river of elemental love, of our oneness, and jump right in, letting it flow over and through you to fill you and become you."

After the journey, the room's energy had changed once again. There was a heady feeling, and each person looked around, remarking on how different everyone looked.

"I can't believe it!" Diana said, looking in a hand mirror after the person next to her remarked on how different she looked. "It's true. I do look pretty, and young, too."

"You're beautiful," remarked Robert. "What a shapeshift."

"There's a brightness in your eyes again," I pointed out. "Have you ever noticed that when a friend is in love, they look fabulous? But we don't have to wait to be in romantic love to have this energy. It is a universal elemental energy, and it can be tapped at all times. Now let's switch gears and do the same journey, but this time with eyes open, looking into the eyes of a stranger."

They all found partners with whom they had had no previous contact and went through the experience again, while Robert and I drummed.

"It was much harder that way. But it's so great feeling that strength of love with someone else, even with a stranger!" Dave said. "Just pure love energy. I really need to practice that one. I want to live like that!"

"Live in love," I urged them. "What a concept! And that is just what you can all do. Now I ask that each of you go out and access that same energy when talking with someone over lunch, when walking through the grounds, when at the grocery store, when having a disagreement, whether you are with your loved ones or with strangers. Live in love. There is in our heads a seeming duality of personal versus universal love. Now you have experienced that love is a single essential energy, strong and useful. It can be accessed at all times and in many situations. Even in your relationships where love is already present, embracing the concept of universal love will help you to trade attachment for personal commitment."

As we all hugged and broke for lunch, we could see the shapeshifts already happening to us. We were connecting to each other, to spirit, to the land. We had begun to embody our spirits, and they were shining through our eyes, through our demeanors, and through our auras. After packing up my drum, I hugged Robert, breathed a sigh of relief, and thanked him.

"This is what it's all about. This is what gets me up in the mornings. As always, I started today a little nervous and uptight, questioning myself. Why am I here? What do I have to teach? It's always that way right before a workshop. Then spirit steps in, and I don't have to worry, or even do anything. Pashi, Pachamama. Thank you, Pachamama. I feel wonderful."

Learning to Listen to Our Inner guides

When we came back together after lunch, we began to discuss barriers.

Dave said, "I know we are all energy, and I have experienced shapeshifting my energy with intent, but I still feel something that blocks me from reaching my stated goals over and over. What is that?"

Many in the circle nodded in agreement. I responded, "We can begin to see the barriers and learn to break them down by listening to messages from our guides. Connection is enhanced by communing, by dialogue. Listen to the answers, to the messages, in whatever manner they come to you. They can come through dreamtime, through our spiritual body, through our emotional body or feelings, through our mental body or thoughts and imagination, or through the physical world in the form of changes in our body, in the world around us, or in our situations.

"In this next journey," I suggested, "begin to develop a relationship with your shapeshifting guides. Begin to act on the answers that you are given. In all the years that I have been journeying, it has been my experience that I have never been steered wrong by my guides. We have learned to communicate very well and we have a very strong mutual respect. I expect them to guide me truly, and they expect integrity of me. They don't always give me an answer; that usually happens when I am not really ready to hear it. When they do answer, I can trust what they say. At times I haven't acted on the answer, and I have always been sorry. Sometimes acting on your inner guide's advice means going against conventional wisdom. I have found it helpful at such times to remind myself to dance like no one is watching. We all face this duality of inner voices and outer voices. You will learn to follow your inner voice even when it differs from convention. We can also affirm that everyone else also needs to do the same by honoring their ways of living.

"In this next journey, be the energy of your shapeshift, feel what it is like to be living your dream, whether your dream is to be without the tumor, healthy, thin, youthful, vital in the community, passionate, beautiful, successful at work, or dancing in front of an audience. Feel yourself deep in the being of that change, deeply feeling the shifted energy. Then ask your guides what the worst thing about that manifested dream would be."

Mary looked surprised afterward. "I've been afraid," she explained, "afraid of my own power. It sounds silly, but there is power in being thin. Keeping myself overweight has been a way for me to remain invisible. It is a great excuse for so many things. It means that I don't have to take responsibility in love relationships. Strange as it may sound, what I found out is that I was hoping that by being overweight nobody would find me attractive. It was hard for me to accept that not everyone would be attracted to me and to await my mate patiently. It's like being fat lets me think that it isn't about me, it's about my external appearance.

"And it doesn't stop there. Oh, no! My weight held me back from so many activities. What a crutch. This isn't pretty at all. It even meant that I didn't have to take responsibility for my life, for my mission. I don't like finding this out. But now I realize that I don't need to be invisible anymore. I'm ready to be me—to find my power and my mission. My guide helped me realize that I need to be patient, to let go of the specifics of my timetable and vision of my 'ideal' life. I need to be ready to be me at all times. My guide promised to remind me of this and to help me. I promised to open up more to the messages, and to listen."

"My answer was no surprise to me," said David. "The worst thing about finding my mission is that I'll have to do it!"

"I never expected the message I was given," said Barbara. "What could possibly be bad about inner peace? I thought I would come up with the definitive answer that nothing could be bad about it. But that wasn't the answer at all. I found out that I would have to give up my entire identity to get inner peace! I am a victim of child incest, and if I found inner peace I would have to stop defining myself that way, even to myself. If I give up my identity—oh my! Who would I be? That's too scary!"

I sighed, teary eyed. Each time I hear such confessions, I am deeply moved. "Ask your guides for answers to that, too." I advised. "They will help you. Many of us don't want to get well, because we feel that we *are* our stories, our illnesses, our situations. Yet our guides will remind us that we are much more than that. The Shuar are a good example. They meet with every situation—even the scary and difficult ones they encounter often in their jungle home—as a gift and ask for the messages.

"The Shuar attitude about life is mirrored in the way they walk. When we from the North first come to the Amazon, we walk looking down all the time, watching each step, narrowing our focus and perspective and missing the glories around us. We push aside and cut away the brush, trying to avoid contact with everything. When the Shuar walk through the jungle, they do so without looking at their feet. They allow the bushes and trees to brush across them as if they were caresses. Softening their focus, they broaden their perspective and look all around, experiencing their connection to the forest. This is a good metaphor for how we can walk differently through life. Just as the Shuar allow the jungle growth to brush against them as they walk along their jungle paths, they allow the branches across the path of life to touch them.

"We can learn to walk like a Shuar. For we are not defined just by our bodies or our life situations. We are eternal spiritual beings having this physical experience called life. We can embody our spirit and live with that knowing, with that expanded sense of our eternal self. Then barriers will be transformed."

The Fabric of Time

"One of the barriers we all encounter is the duality of time. Is there really a now? Is time punctuate or a flowing fabric? Do both possibilities exist at once? How can we live in the moment and at the same time rise above the moment to keep the broader perspective of our eternal horizon in mind? Our next journey will give us a chance to embrace both.

"I want you to journey back to the energy of your manifested dream. This time ask your guides what effect this shapeshift in your energy will have on all your relations, human and otherwise, now and forever."

Again the energy in the room lifted from the journey.

"I feel that my dream to be pretty and youthful has been validated and energized," remarked Diana. "It is as though it has been accepted; as if even my wish to lessen the bags under my eyes is acceptable. Before I felt so vain, but when I asked how having the bags under my eyes disappear would affect my loved ones, I was told that no shift in energy is isolated. Whenever anything shifts, it affects the entire universe now and forever. We are all one. Physical is connected to emotional, mental, and spiritual. So when I shift with intent, set my dream and change my energy, everything changes. That journey was something else! I saw myself glowing, youthful, happy, bright, pretty, attractive. I saw my family shifting through my new energy. I saw conversations and playfulness. I saw them going out into the world with their bright energy affecting others, like ripples in a pond. Wow!"

"No dream is invalid or trivial," Robert said. Asking your guides how your dream will affect all your relations is a good way to make sure that you are working on a dream and not on a fantasy that you don't want to manifest. Clearly for you this is a beautiful dream, in every way. In my experience, out of one dream others arise, and on and on."

"As a plastic surgeon I am a deliverer of physical dreams," I added. "I have listened to and surgically manifested thousands of physical dreams over the years. I have found again and again that those who devalue their dreams, who think they are vain and wrong to put their energy into that particular dream, fare very poorly after the physical shapeshift. All our dreams are possibility, and all are connected. When we value our dreams and put energy into them honorably, when we listen to the messages and take care to differentiate dream from fantasy, then we can live in ecstasy, knowing ourselves and our energy, and how our individual selves affect the whole. If you haven't figured it out yet, I love paradoxes. We go beyond the seeming duality of ego by developing a strong personal spirit while opening to our oneness.

"We can also learn by watching those around us. They are our mirrors, teaching us about our energy, what we are projecting, where we are wasting energy, where we are trying to suppress energy to keep from projecting it, where we are unbalanced, where we are blocked. This evening, as you engage in your usual activities like dinner, conversation, or play, watch your mirrors. Listen to the messages. Whenever you have an emotional response to anyone or any situation, you will know that it is a mirror, that it has a lesson for you and for how you are managing your energy. The stronger the emotive response, the more important the message, and the more you should direct your attention to it and listen to the message."

We stood up and held hands, performing a ceremony to close the sacred circle for the night, giving thanks for all we had shared and learned, for our lives and opportunities, for possibilities and lessons, and then we bid each other goodnight.

Mirror, Mirror

The next morning, as Robert and I lit the candles and camayed the sacred space, the tribe assembled, eager to share and to move on. The shapeshifts were already manifesting in many ways. Woody, an eager part of the community, was involved in a deep discussion with Dave, talking animatedly about some ideas that had come to him in the night. As he described what he would put his energy into, there was a passion in his voice that had been missing just one day before, when we had begun the workshop as "strangers."

"How much difference one day can make," Robert observed. "We thought of ourselves as strangers yesterday, and we all had our fears and our walls. What an illusion! Now look at us," he said, turning and hugging the person next to him lovingly. "How can we ever think of anyone as a stranger if we are all one?"

"Everyone looks fabulous!" I remarked. "Did you sleep well?"

Nodding, many of them mentioned the vivid dreams they had had and the messages they had received.

"I had some doozy mirrors, and some strong messages," Peggy stated. "At dinner in the dining hall I took my plate to a table where there was an open seat, and a couple across from me began to argue. Or should I say that one of them began to argue. She was getting more and more heated and angry as she tried to make her way of thinking heard. I felt like she was trying to win by making the other person give in and admit that she was right. She was so pushy, even mean. Or righteous. I found myself becoming more and more disgusted.

"Then I suddenly remembered what you had said and realized that if I was having a strong emotional response, then this was a mirror. I opened myself up to listen to the message and asked my inner guide for help. My guide told me that if the woman was a mirror, then I had that righteous tendency myself. In the next instant my guide let me know that if I was disgusted by that part of my personality, then I was expending a great deal of energy to try to keep it hidden. In a flash I also saw that the more I fought it, the bigger it got; what I thought I was suppressing everyone could see in my energy, in my demeanor, in my words, in my actions. My guide instructed me to let go, to let my energy flow, to keep my intent clear, reassuring me that as I did so, my fear would subside. I am afraid of myself more than anything else! What a waste of energy! Think how much more energy I will have available to me, and how much clearer I will flow, if I let go of the fear of being me."

"Great lesson!" I said. "All of us will get this lesson in one form or another, again and again. Keep watching for the mirrors that let you know about your energy, and where it is being blocked or wasted. In this way we learn to put our hands on the steering wheel and drive our energy consciously with intent. *Be* your energy, never *become.* That is a key to shamanic shapeshifting."

"I had a different experience," Barbara said. "I went to see a talk last night, and the man was awesome in every way. An avatar. What brilliance of wisdom and light! He was an enlightened being in every way I ever imagined. I was truly in awe, and it scared the pants off me when I thought of him as a mirror! I can't even begin to handle the notion that my strong response indicates that I have that possibility too—I have that energy, and I am blocking that in myself! I can't tell you how much fear that fills me with. I was shaking as I left the lecture hall. The responsibility it holds! The shame of blocking that all my life."

"Ah yes, it is so true that our so-called positive mirrors fill us with more fear than our negative ones do," I explained. "We are deathly afraid of our power, and we sabotage ourselves in so many ways to avoid letting our energy flow. Pay special attention to situations or people whom you admire, whom you are in awe of, and who fill you with envy or jealousy. These mirrors hold very important messages. Listen carefully, and remember to ask spirit for help."

Balancing Male and Female Energy

"Now we are going to work on balancing our energy. Life is full of paradoxes and dualities. For every yin there is a yang. There are many ways that we can be out of balance, and many ways we can find balance. In the next journey, let us look at the duality of gender. I want you to journey to the gender that you are not in this life. If you are a woman, be the energy of a man; if you are a man, be the energy of a woman. We all have both energies within us. Ask where you are unbalanced in your gender energy, what you are blocking, or what you are overexpressing, and how you can become effectively balanced. Ask what is useful to you about that gender energy. Then switch. Journey to the gender you are in this life, and ask the same questions. This will help you play life fully in the gender blessed to you in this life and also open to the opposite gender energy within you."

Walking around the room drumming, Robert leaned over and whispered to me that even though they were lying down in trance, he could visibly see the women's energy becoming harsher, more edgy, and the men's becoming softer.

Sharing in circle afterward, everyone had something to say this time. Reflecting that gender imbalance is a big energy block in our culture, all agreed that there was much to learn. We spoke of the Shuar and their gender balance, their cultural division of labor and valuing of both genders. We spoke of Jempe the Hummingbird, the Shuar god who maintains the male/female balance at all times.

"I'm going to call on Jempe to help me," Peggy said. "I found that I could use my masculine warrior energy to help me walk through my fear. What I learned when I slipped into my masculine side was that my dream is not to be without fear. Fear is a feeling, and a useful one. What I want is to walk through my fear when I feel that I need to."

"I didn't like my feminine energy," Dave said, "she was quite a martyr. Reminded me of my grandmother. She used to get her way all the time while complaining of all she had to put up with."

"These are great introductions to the next two journeys," I replied excitedly. "I just love it when spirit directs the workshop so smoothly. I believe these journeys will be very helpful to you both in finding balance.

"You are going to retrieve some guides for yourselves. This is just a suggestion, of course—something completely different may come to you, and that's fine. But I want to describe the retrieval that will be the intent of these journeys. In the first I want you to retrieve your warrior guide and your compassionate guide. In the second I want you to retrieve your counselor and your wild guide. Often different guides like to help with different issues."

"That was too cool," announced Diana afterward. "My compassionate guide was very different from how I imagined she would be—quite fierce. And the warrior was gentle and wise."

"I noticed something weird, too," said Woody. "My counselor seemed to be very close to my wild guide, like they worked together or something. I didn't expect that at all. To my mind, my wild tendencies have always been in direct opposition to what I thought was right according to my conscience."

"Yes," I said, "that's another duality to consider—the duality of the judge and the madman or madwoman. In her book *Meeting the Madwoman*, Linda Schierse Leonard speaks eloquently of this duality in all of us. When either of these archetypal energies is ignored, they both grow exponentially in severity, one in the conscious and one in the subconscious. When we acknowledge both as part of us at all times, we can listen to these guides and they become balanced. I have found that when they get in balance within us, they are no longer the judge trying to cage the madperson and the madperson trying to kill and annihilate the judge, but become the counselor and the wild one working in concert with our soul's path. Similarly, when embraced and balanced, the dominator and the victim become our warrior and compassionate one. When I find balance, these guides—these energies that are a part of me—can work together effectively in every way. When they become unbalanced again, and I find myself slipping into the victim or the judge, I take a moment to connect again with my guides for help."

"Now I understand my dream last night," Barbara said. "In my dream I was being chased by a huge gorilla, but when I finally turned and faced him, he became an angel who took me on his lap. He looked very fierce, but I could feel his compassion deeply. It was a very healing experience for me."

"Yes," I answered, "the fierce gorilla was a compassionate warrior. When the dualities of the universe come to my attention, I search for ways to best understand and express these seeming paradoxes. The answer that has come to me over and over again is that the way is not to find a 'middle ground.' It is not to find a way to stay in the middle of the extremes of the spectrum, not the moderation of expressing neither pole of the duality. It is to embrace both, fully being both ends of the spectrum at once. For an example, the power and healing of this way of being is felt deeply when you embody your spirit physically to live a fulfilling spiritual life, connecting with spirit and receiving cosmic wisdom every moment while connecting sensually with your body and its surroundings and taking action in your physical life."

Embracing the Shadow

"Another duality we face within ourselves and in our relationships is that of power versus vulnerability. But we need both. You must find what works for you, but I suggest that you open to the possibilities of embracing the dualities of life instead of putting so much energy into fighting them."

Dave looked puzzled. "Isn't that confusing? As a man, I have felt a need to be strong. And I find it scary to feel vulnerable."

"Instead of rejecting your vulnerability," I said, "try diving into it; you may be surprised, as I was, to discover that it can be a way to gain assistance in the form of your subconscious and communal consciousness, whether you find assistance from God, from your physical and nonphysical guides and teachers, or from your inner voice. When I ask my guides in journey about many of the dualities of existence, the way of enlightened being seems clearer, not, as one might surmise from the nature of opposites, confusing. Over and over again I have been given very similar answers to the questions of opposites, such as the duality of light and dark energies.

"As we began to see in the lessons from our mirrors, when our shadow side or dark side is acknowledged rather than repressed, it does not strive for attention by growing large and extreme in our subconscious. I found that I had held my shadow in poor esteem for a long time, repressing that energy. So at first it was essential to direct this part of myself very carefully by continually reassessing and clarifying my dreams and differentiating dream from fantasy. With the help of my guides, I worked to set very clear intent and develop a strong will. And I discovered that this is a path to being able to live with all of one's energies, both light and dark. When you embrace your shadow, it becomes an ally to your soul's will."

"I think that was the most profound lesson I received from the earlier workshop," Woody said. "In fighting my cancer, I needed to stop fearing death. Strangely, by accepting death, more healing energy came into my life."

"Yes," I said, "at the last moment death will come as a friend to us all. By not waiting until the final moment but acknowledging your death as a friend and ally now, you can live life fully without fear. Balancing these opposing energies of which we and all of the universe are made has been for me a very important part of finding true healing."

The circle discussion was animated and passionate as they all began to explore the possibilities of being all of their energy, all the time, all at once. Everyone was still pondering these new possibilities as we made our way to the lake.

Walking through the campus of the Omega Institute in upstate New York, it is easy to forget that you are in the world's most industrialized and busy nation. The gardens are filled with healing plants, the forest is home to myriad birds and animals. Frequent altars are set up as areas for meditation and sanctuary, and the lawns are spotted with groups of people in quiet conversation or individuals in deep meditation. Everywhere there is a feeling of harmonious community; the energy of the countless teachers and avatars fills the air. The lake has a very special energy. The water is home to waterfowl and fish, and the sandy beaches have witnessed and been host to ceremonies of many traditions, leaving a sacred ambience as conducive to reflection as the mirrorlike surface of the lake itself. Here we formed our circle once again and journeyed to our guides to ask about the dualities of life—life and death, vulnerability and power, light and dark, yin and yang. Keeping the quietness of our tranquility, we then closed the circle and took our leave for the night.

Embracing the Starting Point— Readying the Self for True Healing

The morning arrived bright and sunny. A cool breeze caressed us all as we made our way to the room where we were holding the workshop.

"Let's go outside this morning," Robert suggested.

"A grand idea," I replied, and everyone agreed. "It's possible to journey and ask questions wherever you are, by yourself or with a group, inside or outside, with the drum or without. I use the drum to hold the group together as you begin your journey practice, but I don't want you to think the drum is necessary. Sometimes we need help fast. It wouldn't work if I had to stop and pull out a drum in the operating room or in a business meeting, would it?"

We settled on a hill facing the morning sun and sat a while, quietly connecting with the land, the elements, and the spirits around us, enjoying the morning.

"Before we can start any true shapeshift," I began, "we must accept the place where we are beginning. We start with honoring and giving gratitude for our energy, our bodies, our lessons, our situation, our planet as it is now. We must accept, and come out of denial.

"Feel the sun, father Inti, filling you with energy and warmth. Feel the power. Everything that you are, all your energy, came from the sun—without fail, every day, rising and filling the plants with energy that is passed on through the food chain to become all that is you. Feel this and accept this gift, giving thanks for all that you are, all that you have been, and all that you ever will be. Feel the warmth and energy fill you today with the power to be you.

"Feel the earth beneath you, Mother Earth, Pachamama, supporting you in every way; feel the earth that is you. The energy of the sun gave form and substance to the piece of earth that houses your soul as you grew from a one-celled organism to the complex body that you are now. Feel your eternal spirit in your finite body house made of Mother Earth, and give thanks.

"Now feel your face with your hands. Feel the shape, the story written on your face. Feel your eyes and all they have seen. Look inward at yourself and send love to the you that is now. Feel your neck that has faithfully held up your head, day after day, from the day you were born; feel your shoulders that support the weight of all that your story bears and that move your arms, faithfully, day after day, from the day you were born; feel your chest that houses your heart, that holds your emotions and sends the blood around your body to pick up oxygen and nutrients; feel your pulse, your rib cage, your lungs; take a deep breath, feel the life-giving breath housed in your chest, moved by your diaphragm, inflating your lungs, faithfully, every moment of every day, from the day you were born . . ." We went through each area of our bodies, accepting all of the earth that houses our souls, and gave thanks.

"Until now I didn't appreciate my body at all," said Barbara. "There was so much I didn't like about my body, and since I've developed cellulite, I have actually hated my thighs. I cover them up always, even on hot summer days. I've disliked them so much, I've denied their very existence."

"Now I see my face and my eyes as gifts," said Diana, "but more than that I see the bags under my eyes and the lines around them as my story—what I tell myself and others about my life. They are the things that I won't let go of, and in some cases they are the events that I am proud to have survived. They are my badge of honor."

"That was great," Woody said, giving a big sigh. "I didn't know until just now how much I was denying my own body, how angry I was that I had this body that was failing me, that went through the misery and pain of cancer. I didn't want it! And I certainly didn't feel grateful. And yet, this cancer shook me out of a sleepy life and brought me to places and friends I might never have had. And my body has continued on and on through it all, unfaltering, and will do so until the day it stops housing my soul and returns to the Mother Earth from where I began."

"Denial is a very powerful block," I laughed, remembering the many times I had been in denial. "Watch for its return, for we are used to denial habitually. I knew a woman once who was a great healer, a worldwide teacher, in fact. She came to me as a patient with a lump the size of a cantaloupe on her leg. It had been growing at an alarming rate over the previous year. All the while, despite her amazing intuitive and healing abilities, she could not or would not accept what was happening to her body. Knowing that it was a huge cancer, I asked her what she saw when she scanned her own body."

I went on to describe our conversation.

"'I can't see anything,' she said after a time, frustrated. 'I can scan yours.'

'No, keep trying. What is that on your leg?' I asked.

'Oh that, it's just a blood clot. I hit my leg there a year ago. I don't know why it keeps growing.'

'Then why did you come to me?' I asked.

'So you can take it off,' she explained.

'It's not so easy,' I countered. 'Before any surgery we need to know what it is, what the extent of it is, and what it involves other than skin.'

'Well, why can't you do a biopsy?' she asked.

'I think that's a good idea,' I continued, 'but a biopsy is a question, and you should never ask a question that you don't want the answer to. Do you want the answer? Do you know what that answer might be?'

She looked like the blood had drained from her body, at the precipice where denial could no longer hang on. Then she visibly relaxed, her body becoming pink, warm, and more vital than I had seen it be in a very long time. She smiled sweetly.

'Yes, now I'm ready.'

Only then could she begin to work on that cancer. She is a very powerful healer indeed, but in denial she could do nothing, she couldn't even begin to heal. Once she shed her denial, she could listen to the messages that were being given to her. Later we talked many an evening and well into the night about the knowledge gained from this experience, and she started down the road of true healing."

We took time to reflect individually on what true healing would mean to each one of us before taking a break and returning to the room.

Creating a Supportive Environment

Once inside, we began to work on creating a supportive environment. "Even when we shapeshift to a new way of being, when we change our energy," I began, "and gain a new shape, old patterns often return. We have taught everyone around us who we are through the years; we have a familiar energy and habitual patterns of relating to their energies. So we slip back into old patterns easily. That is okay. When you see it happening, don't beat up on yourself. Simply clarify and reset your intent, and be the shapeshift again. Have compassion for yourself and others. Slowly the shapeshift will become the familiar energy, and it will be easier to be that than the old pattern.

"Our environment has a lot to do with our energy. We relate to all the energies around us, and all the remembered patterns. Creating a supportive environment is important in maintaining a difficult shapeshift.

"I can give you an example. When the Chinese invaded Tibet, and many monks fled to live in exile, they did so to maintain their way of life, their values, their ways of being, their energy. When they fled, they took sacred objects with them—thangkas, mandalas. Most of their possessions had to be left behind, but even in the temporary tent camps in exile they surrounded themselves with the images and objects that supported them in their dream of remaining Tibetan Buddhists. Journeying into their beautiful mandalas, they returned to their land in spirit daily, and they transported their way of being to their new lands, supporting the shape and energy that was the dream of their life physically, communally, and spiritually.

"Similarly, we can surround ourselves with a supportive environment in our homes and places of work by bringing in sensual experiences that support the energy we are trying to maintain. Whether it is incense, images, objects, colors, tastes, music, or the written or spoken word—think of what you can use to build a good support system when you get home, and add to it and adjust it as necessary.

"Here at this workshop, we are going to ask spirit for assistance by journeying to ask for a shapeshifting logo."

"A logo?" Peggy asked, laughing. "Like the Nike swoosh?"

"Yes. Think how much that little swoosh brings to mind through its immediate association with words and images carefully chosen by the company—'Just do it,' determination, possibility, activity, fun—all in a logo. You can effectively pack a lot of supportive clout by associating complex ideas with a simple logo; then just the thought of that logo can bring the energy of your shapeshift rushing back whenever you feel yourself slipping. Some logos are amenable to being placed around the areas you frequent physically, and in this journey we are going to do that in alternate reality. When a logo comes to you in the journey, put it in areas that you frequent. Do this now in alternate reality—in your bedroom, bathroom, kitchen, car, workspace—wherever you spend time."

After the journey, Woody was dying to share his experience.

"As I mentioned, this is my second time at this workshop. Last year I had the dream of vitality after the diagnosis and treatment of my cancer. At that time I had been recently diagnosed with colon cancer," he explained to us all a little sadly. "Although I can truly say that I have always marched to my own drummer and have always had a very special connection to spirit— feeling guided and blessed no matter what the experience—this one got me down. I didn't feel like the same person. I wanted vitality! I wanted to live life fully!"

Smiling at the long faces around the circle, he went on. "I went through the operation and started the chemotherapy, but there came a point when my guides told me that the chemotherapy had done what it could, and that continuing further would only begin to damage the non-cancerous tissues of my body. So I stopped, and my doctors were pretty upset, I have to tell you. I felt okay physically, but the experience had wiped me out emotion- ally—I had lost my passion, my spark.

"At this same workshop last year I clarified my dream as one of vitality, but it wasn't until this stage in the workshop, when a logo came to me, that I really felt what that meant to me. My logo was Indiana Jones, Indie for short, and I could feel his energy in my bones. After the workshop I took a sabbatical and went on an archeological dig in the Southwest. Every morn- ing I would face the sun and set my intent, feeling the energy of my shapeshift and journeying. It didn't take long. It was miraculous. I even got the girl! Yes, I was living a vital life in all ways, Indiana Jones with passion and vitality. I had it all.

"After the dig I returned to the East Coast and began teaching again at a college. I even taught some shapeshifting to the students who were interested, and they were so powerful. What naturals! The messages they got! The shapeshifts they achieved! In teaching again, I felt full of vigor and vitality, but the joy of sharing my shapeshifting experiences and watching these kids empower themselves to set their energy and lives with intent brought me back here a second time. I know the steps to take and could have done it on my own, but the nature of my dream begged for a tribe. Now my dream is community, to bring my vitality into community, to be a vital part of community. The logo that just came to me is the Jedi knight. I can feel the energy rush through me even as I speak."

"Woody, you did it again," Robert remarked. "You are a master shapeshifter. I'm so glad you came to share that with me, with us. It warms my heart."

"Did anyone else get a logo?" I asked. "I know that most people get an object, shape, or color, but Woody's experience is really helpful. Even I can get the energy out of his logos."

"I got a seed," Dave said, "and a shovel. My mission seems to be to plant seeds, in every way."

"I got a heart," Diana stated, "and I'm going to put them everywhere to remind and support me."

"Mine was a waterfall," Barbara told us.

"My logo is a bear," said Peggy.

"Mine is a sheep," said Mary, "and that is more funny than you can imagine."

She then went on to recall the time when she was on her honeymoon with her now estranged husband. They were in Ireland with relatives, and they were never alone. Getting in their tiny rental car, they drove to the middle of a field and began to make love.

"After a while the car began to rock back and forth. Now I had heard of love rocking your world, but this was something else. I looked out the window, and there was a herd of sheep walking around and even over the car, and the shepherd walked by and just tipped his hat and went on. We were the talk of that village!" Laughing, she went on, "But now my marriage is all but over, and I think I need to regain that sense of young silliness, and my sense of humor. I think I'm going to need it in the coming year."

We paired up again to do healings on each other, to help each other to remove blocks, and to gain energy and balance. We all went outside and journeyed to the spirit of the plants on the grounds, gathering those that asked to be used for the purpose. The sun was low in the sky, and the moon was already rising. The air was filled with the scent of honeysuckle and the sound of cicadas. Feeling a deep connection with the elements, with the land, and with our guides, we were ready to explore healing.

Using the elements, we brushed our partners with plants, camayed with wine, cologne, and water, covered our auras with incense and burning herbs, and massaged each other with stone huacas.

I was kneeling over Mary, using my huacas in healing, when she sat bolt upright.

"It's gone! Completely gone."

"What's the matter, Mary? What's gone?"

"Nothing's the matter. The pain is gone," she said excitedly. "You see, I came to lose weight, and I have been working on that. I never thought there was hope for this! I have fibromyalgia. I'm an R.N., and I was diagnosed several years ago with this chronic pain condition. Mine has been pretty severe. I have to wear splints and have had every treatment available, to no avail. And suddenly, I feel totally different. I'm not kidding, there is no pain at all. I haven't felt like this for years!"

After the healing she began to cry, something she admitted she hadn't done since childhood. She received a clear message that her fibromyalgia was emotional pain that she was holding in her body.*

We said goodnight, holding each other's dreams close in our hearts. The next morning we met excitedly to share all that we were feeling and being.

---

*Mary's pain relief was complete and enduring. After the workshop, she continued to cry for three months. When her divorce papers were served the next year, she began to feel pain again, but she knew that it was important to acknowledge, feel, and release the emotional pain instead of holding it in her body. She has been well since and has gone on to learn vibrational healing as a way of life.

The Tibetan Star Journey—Embodying Your Dreams

"This morning we will learn an ancient Tibetan journey, the star journey. It was brought out of Tibet by Marina Bellazzi, an Italian shamanic healer, a student of Tibetan shamanism, and the originator of Dream Change's Italian sister organization, The Padma Society.*

"There are three parts to this process. One is the journey to send the dream out to the universe in other realities, the prayer, if you will; the other two parts are in this physical reality.

"I will describe the steps. First, sit comfortably. See before you the dark night, the void. Slowly begin to see a star in the distance, coming closer and closer. As it approaches, see it get bigger and brighter. Send out your dream (it could be in the form of your logo) and your guide to the star. Watch as they coalesce and become one bright shining star. The star comes closer and enters you through your third eye, between and a little above your eyebrows. See the dream-star in your mind, and imagine it as in a huge cave filled with crystals and mirrors that magnify it a million times. Then see it explode! As it explodes, feel the dream flow through everything that represents your mental body, your nervous system, your spinal cord, your thoughts, your stories, your plans, your ideas. Watch as the dream-star returns to the cave that is your cranium and coalesces again in the huge cave, magnified a million times over. Watch it explode again! And again feel it flow through all that is your mental body. Watch it come together again and explode a third time, then see it coming together again in the cave that is your mind.

"Now watch and sense it drop to your throat area, where you can see the dream-star in a huge cave of crystals and turquoise, and watch it explode and coalesce three times, each time becoming one with all that is your will. Then watch as it drops to your heart, a huge cave of crystals, mirrors, and emeralds in your chest, and again watch it explode and come together three times, each time flowing through all that is your emotional

---

*For more on Marina Bellazzi and the origins of the Tibetan Star Journey, see *Shapeshifting* by John Perkins (Destiny Books, 1997).

body and heart, your arteries, veins, emotions. Then watch as it drops to the area just below the belly button and again watch it explode and coalesce three times, each time becoming one with your self that you are in this life, with your identity, personally and tribally, with your ego. And now watch as this dream-star goes up again, through your heart, through your throat, through your mind, and out through your third eye into the cosmos."

"There are many variations of the star journey," Robert continued. "All are equally powerful, and you may be directed by your guides to vary it in some way for yourself. Do this journey at least three times a week. You don't necessarily need drums, you can be anywhere to do it, and time is immaterial in journeying. I have done it in seconds at times."

"It's incredibly powerful," Woody added, "way beyond my greatest hopes. I make a habit of beginning each day facing the sun and doing this journey. That's what works best for me."

"Remember, there are two more parts," I went on. "The second part is to commit to take action, to do at least one thing, no matter how small, in this reality to forward your dream every day.

"The third is to express your dream. Speak it in conversation, not as a maybe, but as a surety. Whenever you get a negative response—that it is an impossibility or can't be done—counter that there are many things that seemed impossible in times past that are sure things now.

"The way you will express your dream and take action will vary depending on what you are working on being. If you feel uncomfortable voicing it to other people at first, speak your dream to the wind, the forest, the clouds, your dog or cat. You can express your dream in many ways other than the spoken word. You can sing it, dance it, or paint it. There are as many form of expression as there are sentient beings in Pachamama."

Then, as we held hands and prepared to say good-bye, I spoke a few closing words about maintaining our faith as we took the lessons and insights of the workshop back into our lives:

"With faith, the world is as we dream it. Along with our dreams, our intent, there are also grand forces of nature, of 'fate' or destiny. With faith, we can fully experience our lives as they unfold, with grace, and choose to be whatever way we dream. No one can 'make' us happy or sad or angry. When we live in this knowledge and responsibility for our own well-being, we create our lives moment by moment. Be happy, have fun, or be sad if you wish—feel it fully and then release. When we all live by choosing and being, moment by moment, appreciating what life hands us, listening and connecting, feeling our oneness, living in ecstasy, then heaven will be with us, here and now."*

---

*The workshop described here is similar to ones that have been held at centers such as Omega and Esalen by Dream Change Coalition facilitators, including John Perkins, Ipupiara, Cleicha, Mary Tendall, and Lyn Roberts-Herrick. Many of the techniques are those of John Perkins, and many have been taught to me by shamans throughout the world. Every workshop is different, and the techniques are modified by the direction of spirit and by the tribe that is the circle at the time. The participants described here are composites of actual workshop participants.

EPILOGUE

Coming Home to the Great Mother

May 1999, India

"THE STUPAS REPRESENT THE FIVE ELEMENTS," Shruthi was saying, as we walked past one of the many Buddhist stupas in Ladakh, a city of her native India. "The base of the stupa—square and solid—represents the earth; the hemispherical next layer—fluid and unstable—represents water; the conical shape represents fire; followed by the half moon, air. The smaller sphere at the summit is the symbol of the fifth element, space or ether, representing the expansive soul, conscious and subconscious."

Struck once again by correspondences in belief in widely separated parts of the globe, I said, "The concept of the fifth element is very similar to that known among the Yachaks as *ushai*, the communion of all the elements, the essence of ecstasy, of our oneness." I once again found myself walking along the path of my life with Shruthi, just as I had on the day of my initiation into the circle of Yachaks. "Shruthi, do you remember the day of the ceremony at the sacred springs, the initiation?"

"Yes, this mountain vista was bringing back memories of that day to me, too," she replied. Much had transpired since that day in Ecuador. I was performing shamanic healings and I was still practicing medicine. More and more I found myself called to teach and to facilitate the healing of the feminine, through workshops in shapeshifting, in healing, in finding beauty without surgery. I continued to lead explorations of individual and collective ways to heal our global community by transforming ourselves, our culture, our dreams.

Shruthi and I had come on a Dream Change trip to Buddhist northern India, land of the ancient Bon shamans and the area where Jesus reportedly studied and taught during his so-called "lost years." There is no reference in the Bible to Jesus's whereabouts between the ages of 12 and 29, but there is evidence that suggests he spent a good number of those years in the area where we were walking.*

Once again I was unsure about why I had made the trip. It wasn't sensible. I had struggled for months, one day deciding to go, the next day deciding against it. I had been torn between this journey that called to me and my home, acutely aware of how much I would miss my children and granddaughters. Yet I knew that there was a reason. Now that I had come, I felt very much as I had that day years before when I wondered why I found myself in Ecuador. I felt the connection between the two trips, the synchronicities.

We had come with Paula, my chiropractor and now cherished friend who had told me about the trip to Ecuador that introduced me to Dream Change Coalition. Her broken ankle had prevented her from going and had allowed me a seat. On this Dream Change trip to India, she was to be married. When her ankle had healed and she finally went to Ecuador, Paula had met her soul mate, Mitch, a psychiatrist and M.D. Now, after more than two years of planning and preparation, they were to be wed. Many of us who worked for Dream Change Coalition as volunteers, sharing a common commitment and passion, had come to honor their union in marriage. Their unfaltering love was to be celebrated in a time-honored ceremony at a Sikh temple in Delhi, the air filled with the scents of jasmine and roses.

The trip was set up as a shapeshifting workshop in the Himalayas, a

*Documented in *The Lost Years of Jesus* by Elizabeth Clare Prophet (Corwin Springs, Mont.: Summit University Press, 1987).

workshop that I would be teaching with John Perkins, the leader of the first Dream Change trip I had made years before. I had a sense of coming full circle. And deep within I knew this was going to be another life-changing pilgrimage.

Ladakh, formerly a part of Tibet, is in a dry desert area of the Himalayan mountain range. The Ladakhi people beamed with spirituality. We were greeted at every corner by "julay" ringing out from young and old. *Julay* is similar in meaning to *shungo* in the Andes, *namaste* in India, and *aloha* in Hawaii. Loosely translated as "from my heart to yours," it recognizes the divinity in each, the oneness. I fell in love again—with the people and the land of vast snow-peaked vistas. It was the high holy week of Wesak, the Taurean full moon celebration of the life, death, and enlightenment of Buddha.

After we arrived, we discovered that we were to have an unexpected blessing. The Dalai Lama, the Tibetan Buddhist spiritual and political leader in exile, was celebrating Wesak that year in Ladakh and would be speaking. On that day, we approached an area reserved for tourists, very close to the main pavilion. We were over 11,000 feet above sea level, so the air was thin and the sun fierce. It was cold in the shade, but in full sun we roasted. As I peeled off layers of clothing and searched for sun protection, I soaked in the view and the rising emotions, letting in the sensory delight of a rainbow of colors, images, sounds, smells, and feelings. Tens of thousands of people had gathered: monks, lamas, and rinpoches in their purple and saffron swathes; Ladakhis clothed in woolen dress, the women adorned with silver, turquoise, amber, and coral. Pointed woolen hats dotted the crowds making their way into the compound. Within, a sea of colored umbrellas gave shelter from the flaming sun. Our nostrils were attacked by the acrid smell of burning sod and incense, and our eyes watered from the smoke.

Fighter planes roared overhead, reminding us of the escalating Indo-Pakistani war, the front line being less than 100 kilometers distant. The stark realities of war contrasted with this peaceful field of prayer, meditation, connection, and compassion. I breathed in deeply. The ocean of people around me was chanting of compassion and wisdom, the foundations of Buddhist principle. It was more than an intellectual study; it was a way of being. I felt it deeply, the warmth filling my belly, and my heart sang. Once again I found myself at home, with a deep knowing. Home.

Words wafted through my consciousness. His Holiness the Dalai Lama was speaking in Tibetan, the loudspeaker blaring a Ladakhi translation to the crowds. Within our area, the gentle lilting voice of the English translator soothed our minds and our spirits as he conveyed the Dalai Lama's words of compassion, of global responsibility, of love and wisdom. His message was of the need to go beyond prayer alone, of the importance of monitoring our choices in life. He talked of how we need to begin with our conscious prayers, choosing our reality with careful thought and emotion, and then take the next necessary step—that of responsible action, achieving balance by combining wisdom with compassion.

Slowly the knowing crept into my mind, and from there to my heart and my soul. The Dalai Lama was speaking of our work with Dream Change Coalition, my life's passion. I was filled with the growing realization that this is the work of each and every one of us, of all cultures, worldwide. This is what is spoken of in gatherings across the planet. Various words and concepts are used to describe this dream change—earth changes, the new millennium, the second coming of Jesus, in our hearts this time.

I felt myself lifted, light, at one with this field of seething humanity and with all the elements—the sun that baked my skin, the air that wafted across my body, the majestic snow-covered mountains, the yak butter tea and the sweet cookies being served to the multitudes, the smoke rising from the piles of sod and incense, the rising and falling lilt of the thousands of voices chanting sacred mantras. I was at one with everything around me. Then, as if in trance, I rose to another level, knowing all of us in Ladakh as one with those in the Andes, in the Amazon, in the plains of North America, in the Great Lakes, in the savannahs and Great Rift Valley of Africa, the great cities of Europe and the Far East, with the moon, with the stars. In that moment, I knew that together we were all coming to the understanding that by our individual thoughts and dreams we create the world around us in a very real way, and then find evidence in our perceptions, actions, and reactions to support our particular vision.

Suddenly I was transported in dreamtime to one of my great teachers, Running Water, a Taino man, a *brujo* or witch doctor. A powerful and honorable man, he works tirelessly to heal, to help others, to teach. His own people and ancestors have long been oppressed, so his reality is a world of bitter anger, distrust, and fear. As a witch doctor, he calls to the dark and uses the powerful energy of these terrifying realities to create extraordinary change. Danger surrounds him through this choice, at all times, in all realms; thus, in his view, constant careful protective vigilance is a necessity. Seen through those eyes, everything—his life, his observations, his actions, the world around him, both physical and spiritual—gives him ample proof of this perspective.

I often sat with him, in the same physical space, surrounded by the same spirits, but I saw a different world through my eyes—a world of hope, compassion, trust, and grace. We lived in the same world, with the same spirits and the same visions, but our experiences were very different. Yet we worked with these universal energies with one heart, staying the course of our intent and our missions, directed by our inner voices and guides. I sent him a deep compassionate prayer of support in the path that he has chosen.

From there I found myself journeying to the Amazon, remembering a night of profound healing. The words of Nunqui, the Shuar goddess of Mother Earth, spoke to me as clearly as if the years had never elapsed. I was dancing again in the flat clearing in front of the lodge of the great Shuar shaman Tuntuam. Nunqui told me she had a gift for me. "What is it?" I queried in childlike excitement. "New eyes," she announced. There in the field in Ladakh I understood even more fully the gift of that night in the Amazonian rainforest—it was the gift of perpetual wonder, to see with the eyes of a first-time viewer, always and forever.

I came back into the present and heard the Dalai Lama speaking. He told of his daily endeavors, moment by moment, to direct his thoughts and energy. He told of the effort involved in creating a view of the world always guided by compassion and by understanding the illusion of ego. He talked of how we can change our dream. In his dream, we are all one—all sentient beings are honored as ourselves, even the insects, all beings, for we have all been fathers, children, brothers, sisters, lovers. We have all been flowers, bees, crows, lions, rocks. I had heard this intellectually before, but in that powerful moment of oneness I came to know it by experience.

Synchronicities occur sometimes even when we try to avoid them. For weeks we had been unsuccessfully trying to change our flight plans so that we could stay on in Leh rather than go to Dharamsala. The war with Pakistan was escalating, and there was a waiting list of hundreds for each flight; there were throngs of people every day at the airport vying for a chance to leave the area. Realizing that if we gave up our reservations, we would not be able to get any others, we reluctantly prepared to leave. On the day of our departure, we made our way with great difficulty through the crowds at the tiny airport, crawling under people and through barriers, dragging our luggage and holding onto each other like a human rope chain. Finally our group passed by the security desk into a clearing. There, waiting to board the same flight, was the Dalai Lama! He mentioned our group to his security guards and—making an exception to his planned five days of rest— invited us to his home in exile.

Our band of thirty dedicated shapeshifters, agents of dream change, arrived at the appointed time at his residence in Dharamsala with excitement and anticipation. Walking through the gardens, each of us found ourselves in deep reflection on our personal paths through life, paths now converging with those of each other. Together our paths were leading us through this garden in Dharamsala to a private audience with this humble, childlike, holy man of compassionate intellect, the fourteenth Dalai Lama of Tibet.

I was surprised to find myself feeling nervous in a way that I couldn't understand. As I meandered up the hill, I pondered the manner in which many of the major religions of the world concentrate on worship of a human being such as Buddha, Mohammed, or Jesus. I was struck by the contradiction between the religions and the teachings of these great holy men who emphasized connection with the divine within us all, not worship of themselves. I thought of how these religions differed from shamanism, a more heartfelt earth-based experience of living in ecstasy—not bliss but the spiritual ecstasy or nirvana of our oneness. The ecstasy of shamanism comes not through years of study and deprivation, not through intermediaries. It comes through our experience of oneness moment by moment—this is spiritual personal empowerment.

Later, as I listened to the Dalai Lama, I felt his humility and his greatness, his power and his empowerment. He condoned the work of Dream Change and we spoke of global responsibility, of cultural diversity, of conscious attention to our world and our dreams, of hard work and determination. Before we departed, we filed up to him to be blessed. He giggled and glowed, and as I approached him, I felt his power run through me. At that moment I experienced a timeless perspective of our connection in lives eternal and the spiritual empowerment imparted by that connection. I also was deeply aware of the responsibility of this empowerment. I realized that this was the basis of my nervous fear—through empowerment comes responsibility.

And then—with new eyes—I saw that along with the responsibility comes the connection, the oneness. We are never alone. I let this knowledge wash over me, filling me with strength, and I realized that we were setting forth together, all of us as one community—humanity, the earth, the animal world, the plant world, the spirit world—all one.

Spring 2001, Africa

I bent over and kissed the earth, breathing in deeply the air of the red dust and smoke of my childhood home. I was back in Africa with Barry Gribbin, a former special forces agent, now an author and martial arts instructor. We had come to develop transformational Dream Change trips to the healers of Africa. Somehow it was perfect. Our culture and Dream Change Coalition—represented by two of our most materialistic, obsessive occupations, soldier and plastic surgeon—had come to hear from those who honored spirit in the earth, from those living in ways far beyond materialistic obsession, living in shamanic ecstasy.

Being in Africa was like being in a warm womb. Childhood memories and emotions flooded through me, and I felt a profound release. Before we visited the Bushmen, I met with Vusamazulu Credo Mutwa in South Africa. Credo Mutwa is a high *sanusi* (the highest order of shaman in the Zulu tradition), keeper of Zulu wisdom and sacred objects, and protector of the Zulu people. Author of *Indaba My Children* and *Song of the Stars,* he is renowned around the world for his power as an individual and communal healer, as well as for his skill and passion as a leader, philosopher, storyteller, and artist.

We talked for hours, jumping from subject to subject, about times past, present, near future, and distant future. He spoke of his life as a healer and of his prophecies. Of the coming war and strife involving the United States. He spoke of extraterrestrial aliens, of assistance and of abductions, of crop circles and pyramids. He spoke of past lives and future lives. He spoke of harmony and of a time when money no longer exists as a measure of energy exchange. He spoke of this and of much more, knowledge imparted from the stars.

We sat around his table as he showed me the sacred objects in his care and commented on the plight of the Zulu in modern South Africa. He told me of his concerns as he aged, suffering from diabetes, as is the case with many of Africa's leaders, as well as of his desire to retire. He spoke of his beloved teacher, his aunt, also a sanusi. Though 103 years of age, she still slept on the floor of a small hut with no door.

"One day," he said, "she was awakened by a man standing over her with a knife. 'Why did you wake me up?' she asked. 'To kill you,' the man answered. 'What a stupid reason to wake anyone up!' she replied, pulling the blanket back over her head. 'If you're going to kill me, go ahead and get it over with, but don't wake me up!' You know, that big young man turned and ran fast from my old aunt." Credo laughed long and hard.

Then he sighed deeply. "I am saddened and puzzled," he went on, switching subjects. Holding up a recent *Time* magazine, tears came to his eyes as he stared at the face on the cover whose expression told the tale of the human suffering in the AIDS epidemic. Turning the magazine to the incidence map that graphically told the tale of the ravages of the disease among his people, demonstrating the highest incidence in his land of southern Africa, he asked, "Why? Why are we afflicted so terribly? Why us? I have been all over the world and have seen many people and many ways of life. The people of the Andes, for example, have lifestyles very similar to ours, yet look at the number of cases there," he said, pointing to the bar graph. "My aunt taught me well, and she is also a pushy old woman. She reminds me daily of the oath I took as protector of my people, and she urges me to do something. As an old man I feel that in some way I have failed my people."

Virginia, who was near the end of her training with Credo as a *sangoma*, the Zulu word for shaman healer, joined the conversation. "So many people are dying," she explained, "and the saddest part is the dying culture. Our families, our traditions, are suffering. Everyone is afraid of this virus. Now it is not unusual for those who find out that they are infected to keep this a secret from their family for fear of being shunned. This is not the Zulu way," she bemoaned. "It is Zulu tradition to care for any sick family member. In fact, the whole community helps to care for the sick."

Credo turned and said, "Virginia is right; this disease affects the whole family in terrible ways without even infecting them all. In the traditional way, when someone became ill the whole family joined in caring for that person. Let me show you the clinics I hope to create. I'll draw out the rough plans for you now, a prototype. The idea is to build something cheaply that can be replicated throughout the townships, throughout the land."

He drew his plan on a piece of scrap paper—a simple building with many windows and a veranda so that light and air flow through the main room. There were aromatic plants and water pools with falls so that the sound of trickling water and healing aromas continually caressed the senses. A few beds for the sick person to sleep in were placed in the room, with hammocks strung for the severely ill so that they needn't die in bed. Some areas of the floor would be hard, while others would be sandy so that people could feel the earth under foot, and someone with seizures would have a soft place to fall. He drew huts for the staff surrounding this building, as well as many huts for the families so that they could stay and care for their kin.

"The clinics should not be isolated," he went on. "People who have recovered sufficiently to leave will be asked to return to give hope to those who are more ill."

We went over the drawing and the concepts at length, and then I had a sudden realization. "Baba, you know of course of Hippocrates, said to be the father of allopathic medicine?"

"Yes, I do," said Baba Credo, "the Greek."

"I just realized the similarities. His clinics are said to have been very much like what you have described! It's astounding, really; he lived so many years ago, and his words and ideas have been distorted in so many ways. His clinics were places of deep true healing, more like spas where all the senses were brought into the healing process and where lifestyle was emphasized. You have the same dream as the very father of modern medicine."

"How wonderful! An old Zulu man going back to the roots of Zulu healing ways, and through this bridging the very roots of medicine. Perhaps it is time for true healing all over the world."

He spoke of an old Zulu herbal remedy—a fiercely aromatic plant whose spirit is strong. "This plant spirit gives us great strength in healing," he said gratefully, describing how he and others have used this herbal remedy to help people with cancer, AIDS, and other immune deficiencies with great success. Though not curative, it imbues the patient with a strength of spirit that brings about much needed weight gain, a sense of well-being, alleviation of depression, and general overall improvement. His eyes shone brightly as he spoke passionately about Sutherlandia, about his clinics, about his desperate love and hope for his people.

"Baba, of whom do you speak when you say 'my people'?" I asked of him. "You know that my childhood home is Kenya, yet somehow I can't really claim Africa as my home. I often wonder who my people are and where I can call home."

"A good question," he responded. "I am the sworn protector of the Zulu people by my ancestors' bidding, and I am committed to them in any way that I can help. Yet, my sense of 'my people' also extends to all on this earth, to all colors and races. We are all family in my heart, and the world is our home. Perhaps it is not that you do not belong anywhere, but that you belong everywhere."

I remembered the experiences I had had of being at home in so many places around the globe—with the thousands gathered to hear the Dalai Lama in Ladakh, with the Shuar healers in the Amazon, with the Yachaks high in the Andes, at my home in Maryland. I had come back to Africa this time to create a trip that would bring this concept into the hearts of others. Africa's energy is uniquely earthy, full and bittersweet in its closeness to the physical realities of life and death. Nowhere is this connection more intense than among the Bushmen or San people.

We sat in a circle on the dry dust of the Kalahari. The night desert air was chilling, yet the fire in the center was kept small to preserve the precious supplies of firewood.

The stars shone like a blanket overhead, the Milky Way wiping a stripe through the middle of the night sky. Here in Botswana, near the Namibian border, the village of !Kung San Bushmen lived simply, using hunting, tracking, and gathering techniques passed down through the generations, now bridging the ancient and modern ways by sifting through the shifting sands in the winds of change.

Xashi translated the musical clicks of the Bushmen speech as we entertained each other with endless tales around the fire. The children played while babies slept peacefully in their mother's and grandmother's arms. Some of the elders smoked raw tobacco through shiny metal tube pipes, the smell acrid yet comforting and familiar.

We recounted the events of the day. In the morning we had watched the birth of a baby goat while its mother bleated vulnerably outside Xao Xam's home. Later in the day, one of the most poisonous snakes in the world, the boomslang, had been spotted high up in a tree, resulting in hours of communal work to capture and kill it. The young men laughed as they recounted the time they had spent trying to hit the snake with stones, large rocks thrown freehand and small stones propelled by slingshots. Ultimately the snake was stunned and stopped its journey higher and higher up the tree. One of the young men told of how he climbed up with a long hooked branch to bring the snake crashing, though still wiggling, to the ground. I recalled how the lethally poisonous snake had writhed in the air while Barry held it up to check its identity and condition. The young Bushman who gave the final blow to the head recalled proudly how his blow protected the children of the village from one of the many mortal risks awaiting them daily.

Hearing this story recounted, we all laughed long and loud, remembering our mortal fears and struggles of the day.

Xashi pointed to the sky. "Do you see the arrow?" he asked, pointing to what I had been taught was the sword of the constellation we know as Orion.

"Yes," we replied.

"See the bright star over there? That is the one who shot the arrow, but it fell short of the zebra," he said, pointing to the belt of Orion. "It was aimed well, but it was stopped short by the dark night. We look for the arrow when we are out at night; the direction of its path is north."

My eyes searched rapidly for the Southern Cross to confirm the accuracy of this age-old tale and tool. All eyes around the fire followed in the stars as Xashi told us the tale of the arrow falling short of its zebra mark, of the dark matter in its path, of the ostrich egg at the end of the world that was opened for its life-giving water.

"Thanks, Xashi. Now I'll never get lost at night!" Barry spoke with gratitude for this ancient wisdom that could direct us in the desert night, even at times when his GPS could not get a satellite signal.

"You can't get lost if you don't know where you're headed," pointed out his son Byrne. We all laughed at his joke, and at his wisdom—he had come to understand the joys of existential wandering that the Bushmen had been blessed with in times past.

"Yes," Xashi said, still chuckling, "but now that we have a village, it stays right here always and becomes our destination, even when we go out hunting. Times are changing, that is certain."

I sat pondering our modern scientific models of the universe. New evidence points to the fact that the universe is, after all, flat. I knew from my father of the physicists' struggles through the years to make physical observations of the universe fit with the elegant abstractions of the language of mathematics. They are searching for a unified model of the universe that can explain both gravitational macrophysics and elemental particle microphysics.

As if reading my thoughts, Barry said, "Now scientists are describing the smallest units of the universe as vibrating strings, creating a universe of exquisite resonating orchestral music. Can you hear it?"

I replied, "Much is hidden from our senses. Within the scientific model it has long been accepted that none of our theories make sense without the presence of dark matter, matter that does not emit light. We can't see it. We only know that it exists by our calculations of the speed of orbiting celestial bodies, and those calculations show that it might be as much as eighty percent of the known universe."

Barry asked, "If the validity of the scientific theory of the universe itself depends on the existence of vast amounts of matter that can't be seen or sensed in any conventional way, why is our scientific culture so inflexible when it comes to considering views of the world that depend on empirical rather than measurable evidence, views that depend on a sensing or knowing that defies reason? The stories that we have heard tonight, and those of indigenous people around the globe, describe the deepest mysteries of physical science—the mysteries of dark matter, of a flat universe, of nonlinear time, of multidimensional space-time continua, of the illusory nature of separation, of our oneness, of the holographic universe, of vibrational energy . . ."

"Yes," I said, "it is time to begin to believe what we see rather than see only what we believe. Perhaps those of us from industrialized countries need to listen carefully to the tales told around fires all over the world, to listen to our indigenous elders, and to open to the world around us in all its glory and possibility. If we come to understand that we are all indigenous to this Mother Earth/universe, that she is our shared home, then surely we will treat our great Mother with care and honor."

The village women prepared for the song of the trance dance as the men began strapping on their ankle rattles, which were made from the dried torsos of countless desert beetles. They were sparsely dressed in swaths of bark cloth, and their ocher-smeared bare breasts shone in the firelight.

Around the fire, inside the circular path of beaten dust, the women began to sing and clap. Soon the music surrounded us with a deep, raw, ancient quality that spoke directly to my soul. The blend of harmonic song and syncopated hand percussion traveled far into the night air with the nature and complexity of a full orchestra. The songs told of the kudu antelope, the eland, the ostrich, and the honeybee, and of healing. The men, young and old, continued to stomp rhythmically to the music and danced with rippling muscles as all of us felt pulled into the trance-inducing beat.

I lay on the ground by the fire, gazing at the stars, while the music of the trance dance held me in a deep pensive space. I thought of this isolated San community, a twelve-hour drive from the nearest town, yet changing as surely as the Shuar are changing, as all the other communities of the world are changing, falling into the dream of the industrialized nations in insidious ways.

Suddenly I was startled by a commotion. The elder healer, Xau Xam, had fallen over in deep trance, landing in the fire. Xashi and one of the other Bushmen pulled him out and attempted to keep him safe from burns and thorn bushes. The old Bushman healer lapsed into coma. Suddenly he was up again, going through the community of spectators around the edges, to Bushmen, Herrero tribesmen, and Caucasians alike, chanting and moving us with a rocking to and fro movement, shaking us all with healing prayer and blessings. He lingered long with some whom he deemed more needy of healing, guided by the messages received in trance, and from time to time he fell down again for long periods in coma. All the while the dancing and singing continued, the women also getting up to dance around the circle one by one as the spirit moved them.

The sound flowed strongly through and around me. I joined in clapping and then fell into my own journey of deep healing trance. Journeying to Baba Credo, I thought of the new and ancient clinics holding hope for the family that is our planet, hope for true communal healing.

I thought of my parents. Fay and Marvin had lived a love story surpassing all, married now for more than fifty years, attached to each other even more today than at any previous time, perhaps painfully so. I glanced at my watch and calculated the time at their home in Hawaii, the other side of the earth. My parents were coming to live with me in Baltimore. They would be getting ready to leave with my adult children, Alice and Michael, who had gone—along with my son-in-law, Tim, and James, a friend and an R.N.—to help my father pack up and transport my ailing mother, who had been disabled for many years. She was bedridden, demented, and partially paralyzed from a stroke. Her condition, with all its discomfort and indignity, caused me great pain. It dawned on me that she might be waiting until my dad was well supported and cared for by us before she would be willing to leave this life. I remembered that two years earlier my daughter Alice had said, "Grandpa, do you think maybe Grandma won't die until you give her permission?" "Never!" he responded to her indignantly.

But never comes sooner than we think, and the pain of seeing her deteriorate steadily had become overwhelming for him. Their love for each other was transcending their attachment to this life, to their bodies. After years of coaxing, my dad had finally agreed to leave the dream that was their home in Hawaii. Living on their beloved land for thirty years, they had created a garden of pure passion, growing an unparalleled collection of rare fruit and ornamental trees from seed. Many of the trees now towered above their home—mangosteen, durian, litchees, fehi bananas. The beauty of their garden was the physical manifestation of their dream and of their love for each other. Now they would be packed up, ready to leave the land into which they had poured their hearts. I sighed deeply. It felt as though they would be leaving my mother's soul there in Hawaii.

I still had two weeks in Africa, and I looked forward to the time when I would go home, and to the opportunity to live closely again on a daily basis with both my parents. I understood that it was bound to be difficult, but I knew that the closeness would also be ecstatic. I sat up, awakened by the end of the dance as everyone readied to leave. We were to be up and out of there very early the next morning to drive south to meet with another community of Bushmen near the town of Ghanzi.

Ghanzi was a town of two cultures clashing. The Afrikaaners were a people besieged, hanging on with white knuckles while the winds of change blew fiercely around them. They were used to control and power, and they were letting go of their dreams reluctantly, and at times violently, to the black Africans since the abolishment of apartheid. We arrived after dark, too late to drive beyond the town to our destination in the desert. We searched out the only hotel in town. It was surrounded by iron bars, and we had to drive through heavily guarded gates to get to the protected parking area. Inside, the hotel reeked of decaying gentility. The large colonial bar was silent; no music played in the huge wood-paneled room where impressive stuffed heads stared down at us impassively—kudu, eland, buffalo, impala. From outside the gates we could hear the sounds of drunken urban Setswana partiers. The loud music and the noise of raucous fights drifted through the empty rooms in sharp contrast.

At the front desk of the hotel was a stern Afrikaaner woman, probably in her thirties, but aging rapidly in this time of turmoil. She looked up coldly as I asked for a room. "Do you have a reservation?" she queried.

"No," I replied, looking around to see if I had missed something in the empty halls.

Taking my credit card, she pulled out the heavy registration book to be filled in laboriously, and gave us our room keys.

Soon we were eating dinner in a huge, regal dining hall surrounded by oil paintings of wildlife in elaborate frames, while a line of stiffly uniformed black Africans waited on us with bone china, following obvious strict orders of deportment. We were in a farming region, and the food was delicious. The air, however, was tense.

Afterward, sitting in the still, empty bar, I felt a sudden chill going up my spine, followed by the intense sensation of my mother's energy surrounding me like a warm hug. I felt closer to her at that moment than I had for many years of her illness.

Barry interrupted my reverie. "Your handbag's ringing," he said, pointing.

Grabbing my cell phone, I answered to hear Alice's voice speaking from our home in Baltimore. "Momma, we're home.... She died. Grandma died about fifteen minutes ago ..." and then the phone battery went dead.

Rushing over to the reception desk, I noticed the Afrikaaner woman sitting in the back room beyond the reception area around a table with her family, Grandma Oma, Grandpa Opa, and the children. They were all watching television in the tiny room that was their home, the place of their chosen siege in this, their decaying lifestyle.

"I need to call the United States," I told her. "My mother has just died."

The tension in the air lifted as her cold, hard walls melted, her eyes softening liquid.

"I'm so sorry." She spoke from the heart. "Let me help you."

After the call, she returned, and I explained that I would be checking out.

"Where are you going," she asked, "home?"

"Yes," I said. "Home."

More about Dream Change Coalition

When I first became a member, Dream Change Coalition was a small grass-roots organization working to facilitate the reconnection to our Mother Earth, the remembrance that indeed we are all indigenous to this earth plane, and to change our collective dream to one that honors this.

Since then, Dream Change Coalition has grown exponentially, touching a chord in our communal hearts, a longing for connection, expanding into a worldwide umbrella of multiple organizations working toward the same goals.

In the United States, Dream Change Coalition operates under Dream Change, Inc., with 501 (c) 3 nonprofit status. Through the years the tribe has grown with the passionate energy of many volunteers, like myself. Our core group now meets several times a year as we make our way through this un-Western and unfamiliar attempt at a fluid organization with less hierarchy than any other that I have ever worked for. Our core consists of myself; DCC founder and author John Perkins; Ipupiara and Cleicha, shamans and Ph.D. anthropologists dedicated to Dream Change through their tireless teachings and healing work; Mary Tendall, a psychotherapist who works closely with the Shuar to develop sustainable industries and ways to maintain the traditional knowledge, music, and connection, and who also uses Shuar shamanic shapeshifting techniques to help our culture's wounded warriors, the Vietnam veterans; Lyn Roberts-Herrick, a shamanic Reiki master with extensive training in Buddhist studies and psychology who has forged deep connections with shamans in Siberia and has been instrumental in expanding Dream Change to shamanic communities outside of Ecuador.

Dream Change Coalition is also dedicated to healing, individually and communally, as a way of being rather than as a destination or goal, teaching healing and shapeshifting techniques worldwide. All of the core group are practicing healers and teach healing as a way of being, a way of opening to spirit in the world around us. We work to heal by effecting change in our global community as well. An example of the ways in which we work together is the ePOLE (Pollution Offset Lease for Earth) program, which was developed at a meeting of core DCC people along with many shamans from South America. Through this program, the amount of poisonous greenhouse gasses (CO_2) produced each year by the average United States Citizen, approximately 21 tons, is offset, and forests—along with hundreds of species of animals and plants—are preserved. This is done in ways that honor and empower the local inhabitants of the rainforest, the stewards of the trees. The ePOLE project also raises consciousness, through educational programs, workshops, and media, about the impact our industrialized dream is having on the forests and on of all Earth's inhabitants. When you become an ePOLE supporting member, you also receive free internet services and identify yourself as an agent of change with your (member's name)@dreamchange.org email address.

For more information about Dream Change Coalition, ePOLE, transformational trips to the Andes, Amazon, Africa, and Siberia, healing sessions, and workshops, please visit our Web site at:
    www.dreamchange.org
    or call us at (561)622-6064.

If you would like to make a tax-exempt contribution, please make checks payable to **Dream Change** and mail to:
    Dream Change
    P.O. Box 31357
    Palm Beach Gardens, FL 33420